Defend, O Lord provides an excellent introduction to the practice of confirmation as it is understood in the 1662 *Book of Common Prayer.* Martin Davie supplies a concise and clear summary of the background to the confirmation service, its liturgical development, and the theology that underlies it. There is also a very helpful commentary on the text, and insightful answers to questions that arise about the practice of confirmation. It is a very readable book by a scholar who has mastered the material and made it accessible to a wide audience. I recommend it wholeheartedly.

Justyn Terry, Wycliffe College, Vice Principal and Academic Dean

I wish I had been given a book like this when I became a bishop. Martin explains the meaning of the service in a way helpful to the enquiring candidate and superbly offers to overstretched clergy (and bishops) the reasons why attention to the Prayer Book will resource and shape discipleship making now. I hope his updating of the Book of Common Prayer service will be included as an alternative to that in Common Worship. May many be blessed in their reading of this book who come to confirmation and lay on hands after the manner of the apostles.

Keith Sinclair, Church of England Evangelical Council, National Director

DEFEND, O LORD
CONFIRMATION ACCORDING TO THE *BOOK OF COMMON PRAYER*

MARTIN DAVIE

The Latimer Trust

Defend, O Lord: Confirmation according to the *Book of Common Prayer* © Martin Davie 2022. All rights reserved. Scripture quotations are taken from the Revised Standard Version (1952).

ISBN 978-1-906327-74-3 Published by the Latimer Trust March 2022.

The Latimer Trust (formerly Latimer House, Oxford) is a conservative Evangelical research organisation within the Church of England, whose main aim is to promote the history and theology of Anglicanism as understood by those in the Reformed tradition. Interested readers are welcome to consult its website for further details of its many activities.

The Latimer Trust
London N14 4PS UK
Registered Charity: 1084337
Company Number: 4104465
Web: www.latimertrust.org
E-mail: administrator@latimertrust.org
Views expressed in works published by The Latimer Trust are those of the authors and do not necessarily represent the official position of The Latimer Trust.

Contents

Preface	1
Introduction	3
1. The development of confirmation in the Patristic and Medieval periods	5
2. The development of the confirmation service in the *Book of Common Prayer*	13
3. A commentary on the confirmation service in the *Book of Common Prayer*	45
4. Questions about confirmation today	79
Appendix A: The service of confirmation in *An English Prayer Book*	103
Appendix B: Admission of Baptised Children to Holy Communion Regulations 2006	107

Preface

The Reformers sought to produce new and revised liturgy that expressed Justification by Faith, as Luther had seen that was 'the article of a standing or falling church'. The Gospel, understood in a Pauline and New Testament way, was the filter they passed everything through. That Gospel, which gloriously was about salvation through faith alone, by grace alone, based on the sufficiency of Christ's atoning work for us alone, was their joy and delight.

They therefore saw Confirmation as the necessary catechetical hoop for people to pass through in a church which practised infant baptism. It was essential that everyone was challenged to take upon themselves the promises made for them in their baptism, and to come to a personal saving faith for themselves when of age, and not just to shelter under the faith of others and enjoy the benefits of a covenant relationship with God vicariously. As Luther once said the essence of New Testament Christianity is the ability to use a personal pronoun- 'Jesus is *my* Saviour, He is *my* Lord!' Martin Davie's work is very helpful indeed in showing us very clearly the changes that the English Reformers made to the Confirmation Service to make it fit for purpose - to be a vehicle which encouraged people to come to personal saving faith, and to seek God's help so that they might henceforth live as obedient disciples of their Saviour. I warmly commend it.

When I was a serving bishop, I had one parish that used Confirmation brilliantly. After a Christianity Explained course, when people had been converted to Christ, they were encouraged to be confirmed. I was invited to come and preach the Gospel evangelistically, and at the end say- 'Do you wish you had been confirmed tonight in the light of all that you have seen and heard (including the wonderful testimonies of the candidates)? Well, you can be! The Rector is starting a new course on Monday and I will be back in six months for another Confirmation Service!' By God's grace it was very effective in a rolling evangelistic programme. I hope that due to reading this booklet clergy will be more confident about Confirmation, and its usefulness in gospel work, and that it can, where possible, be used, as I have suggested and the Reformers believed, as a catechetical and evangelistic tool!

Wallace Benn

Introduction

The Christian gospel declares that through the life, death, resurrection and ascension of Jesus Christ, sin, death and the devil have been defeated and a new life in right relationship with God has been made possible for the human race and, eventually, for the whole of creation.

A question that arises from this declaration is how what Christ has done becomes effective in the lives of particular human beings.

According to the ancient tradition of the Church of England, and of the Western Christian church as a whole, a key part of the answer to this question is that there are two rites of 'Christian initiation' through which the benefits of what Christ has done are conveyed to those who respond to the gospel with repentance and faith.

These two rites are baptism and confirmation.

In baptism, by the action of the Spirit, we are united with Christ in his death and resurrection and thereby, as Paul teaches us, we die to our old life of sin and death and rise to a new life with God which will be fully revealed at the resurrection of the dead at the end of time (Romans 6:1–14).

In confirmation we reaffirm the promises which we made (or were made for us) at our baptism, and we receive through the laying on with hands with prayer the sevenfold gift of God's Spirit which was first given to Christ (Isaiah 11:2–3). We are thereby given strength through the Spirit to live the new life we have been given in baptism, and protection from all that would turn us away from God.

Although it is the confirmation services in *Common Worship* that are most commonly used in the Church of England today, the normative confirmation service, to which the *Common Worship* services are authorised alternatives, is the confirmation service in the 1662 *Book of Common Prayer*.

The purpose of this little book is to provide an introduction to, and commentary on, the 1662 service.

Chapter 1 provides the historical background to the 1662 service by describing how the church's understanding and practice of confirmation developed in the Early Church and during the Middle Ages.

Chapter 2 looks at how the confirmation service in the *Book of Common Prayer* developed from 1549 to 1662 and the theological reasons for this development.

Chapter 3 provides a detailed commentary on the *Book of Common Prayer* confirmation service.

Chapter 4 responds to ten questions that are commonly asked about confirmation today.

Two appendixes contain a modernised version of the *Book of Common Prayer* confirmation service and the Church of England's current regulations concerning the admission of children to Holy Communion.

Chapter 1:

The development of confirmation in the Patristic and Medieval periods

The English Reformers inherited a pattern of Christian initiation involving confirmation which developed in the Western Church from the end of the Patristic period onwards.

The Western pattern of Christian initiation in the fourth and fifth centuries

In the fourth and fifth centuries, while there was no single agreed rite of Christian initiation, there was, in the Western Church at least, a broadly similar overall pattern of Christian initiation with many common elements. This pattern involved a period of catechetical instruction followed by testing, prayer and fasting. There was then a vigil, sometimes night-long, at the cathedral church. This vigil normally took place on Holy Saturday or the Eve of Pentecost, and occasionally at other times. Following the vigil, the candidates renounced evil and made a profession of faith. They were then baptised in water in the name of the Trinity by the presbyters assisted by the deacons.

In some places, there were anointings by a presbyter after the baptism and either after these, or directly after baptism, the candidates were taken to the bishop who completed the rite with a prayer for the sevenfold gifts of the Spirit listed in Isaiah 11:2 accompanied by the laying on of hands and/or anointing with the oil of chrism (a mixture of olive oil and balsam used to signify the gift of the Holy Spirit).

In the fourth and fifth centuries, 'baptism' was a shorthand way of referring to all the various elements of this rite.[1] What we would call confirmation was thus part of baptism. From the fifth century onwards, however, three developments took place which led to the dissolution of this single complex rite of initiation, at least in the Western church.

The reasons for the dissolution of the Western pattern

First, infant baptism became the norm. This meant that the traditional pattern of catechesis prior to baptism and personal confession of faith at baptism ceased in the case of most of those who were being baptised. The pattern that replaced it was one in which the personal confession of faith and commitment at baptism was undertaken by parents and godparents on behalf of infants on the understanding that these infants would receive catechetical instruction as they grew up and confess the faith for themselves.

Secondly, the direct link between baptism and admission to communion was broken. Admission to Holy Communion was postponed until infants who had been baptised were old enough to receive the sacrament with a proper degree of understanding.

Thirdly, the growth of the church in Western Europe from the fifth to the eleventh centuries and the large size of many Western dioceses, particularly north of the Alps, meant that it became impractical for a bishop to preside over all the baptismal rites in person.

---

[1] For a convenient compilation of the documentary evidence for the baptismal rites in the Patristic period, see E. C. Whitaker and M. E. Johnson, *Documents of the Baptismal Liturgy*, 3rd ed. (Collegeville: Liturgical Press, 2003).

As a result of these three factors, the final part of the Western baptismal rite, the laying on of hands with prayer by the bishop, eventually became a separate rite. In the Western Church in the Middle Ages there were thus two rites of Christian initiation. The first was baptism, normally presided over by a priest, and the second was what came to be called confirmation, which was presided over by the bishop.[2] The role of the bishops was justified by reference to the action of the apostles in Acts 8:14–17, the bishops being understood as the descendants of the apostles in this regard.

The teaching of Faustus of Riez

The existence of a separate rite of confirmation raised the question of the meaning of this second rite. What came to be accepted as the classic answer to this question was given in a sermon attributed to Faustus, Bishop of Riez in Provence, which is thought to have been preached in about 480 AD. The text for this Pentecost sermon was Joel 2:28, 'I will pour my Spirit upon all flesh.' Using the term 'confirmation' (*confirmatio*) to describe the laying on of hands by the bishop after baptism, Faustus asks rhetorically:

> What good can the mystery of Confirmation do to me, after receiving the mystery of baptism? For, so far as I can see, we have not received the full gift from the font, if, after

---

[2] The term 'confirmation' came to be generally used from the eleventh century onwards, although the term only came to be universally used following the Council of Trent in the sixteenth century.

the font, we need the addition of a new kind (of grace).[3]

Faustus's response is to say that confirmation following baptism is not pointless because it give us the strength we need to lead the new life we received at baptism and to do battle against the forces of evil.

> That it is not so, dearly beloved, let your kindly attention be given to me. For military discipline thus demands, that when an emperor has received any man into the ranks of his army, he should not only put his mark on the man, but also equip him with fitting arms for the battle. So in the case of a man who has been baptised, that Benediction (i.e. of Confirmation) is a means of defence ... The Paraclete is a Keeper, a Comforter, and a Protector for those regenerate in Christ. Therefore, the Holy Ghost, Who descends upon the waters of baptism with his saving inflowing, bestows His fulness in the font for restoring innocence; while in confirmation He grants an increase for progress in grace. And because in this world we must walk all our days amidst invisible foes and dangers, therefore in *Baptism* we are *regenerated* unto life, *after baptism* we are *confirmed* for our conflict; in baptism we are purified, after baptism we are strengthened; and so

---

[3] Text in A. Theodore Wirgman, *The Doctrine of Confirmation* (London: Longmans, Green & Co., 1902), 253.

the blessings of regeneration suffice in the case of those who immediately pass away from life, but in the case of those who have to live their lives the aids of Confirmation are necessary.[4]

On the basis of a mistaken attribution to the fourth-century Pope Militiades, Faustus' sermon was included in Gratian's *Decretum* (c. 1140) which became an important source for Western canon law and throughout the Middle Ages it was the standard explanation of the meaning of confirmation. As we shall see in chapters 2 and 3 of this study, it is also the understanding of confirmation reflected in the *Book of Common Prayer*.

The understanding and practice of confirmation in the Middle Ages

Because confirmation had thus become a chronologically separate rite from baptism, with a theological significance of its own, it came to be regarded in the Middle Ages as a distinct sacrament. There were thus two complementary sacraments of Christian initiation, baptism and confirmation.

For example, in 1439, The Council of Florence ruled that 'there are seven sacraments of the New Law, viz, baptism, confirmation, the eucharist, penance, extreme unction, orders and marriage.' It went on to say that 'through baptism we are spiritually reborn; through confirmation we grow in grace and are strengthened in faith.'[5]

---

[4] Wirgman, *Doctrine of Confirmation*, 253–54. Italics in the original.
[5] Texts in J. H. Leith, *Creeds of the Churches*, rev. ed. (Oxford: Basil Blackwell, 1973), 60–61.

As Gregory Cameron notes, the administration of the sacrament of confirmation was seen as involving 'prayer by the bishop over the candidates, the anointing of candidates on the forehead, and the laying on of hands and signing with the cross' with the most essential element (the 'matter') increasingly viewed as the 'the anointing with Chrism by the Bishop.'[6]

Although the pattern that developed in the Western Church was thus for the priests to baptise and the bishops to confirm it was known, that in the Eastern Church there was different pattern of initiation in which there was no separate confirmation, but in which those who were baptised were instead 'chrismated' by parish priests with the use of chrism blessed by a bishop. In 1351 a decree by Pope Clement IV recognized this practice as equivalent to Western confirmation and stated that the See of Rome could give permission for a priest to administer confirmation using chrism prepared by the bishop. The teaching of this decree was reiterated by the Council of Florence – and the same idea was also taught by Thomas Aquinas.[7]

At the end of the medieval period the Council of Trent anathematized those who denied that the bishop was the ordinary minister of confirmation, but deliberately did not condemn the idea that a priest might act as an extraordinary minister of confirmation.

---

[6] Gregory Cameron, 'The Development of Confirmation and its relationship to Admission to Communion' in J. Conn, N. Doe and J. Fox, eds., *Initiation, Membership and Authority in Anglican and Roman Catholic Canon Law* (Cardiff: The Centre for Law and Religion Cardiff University; and Rome: Pontifical Gregorian University/ Pontifical University of St. Thomas Aquinas, 2005), 74.
[7] Thomas Aquinas, *Summa Theologiae*, Part III, Q.72.11.

Although children were confirmed in infancy, there was a trend in the Middle Ages towards deferring the rite to a later age. This was partly because bishops were not readily available and because confirmation was not viewed as necessary for salvation in the way that baptism was. Eventually, the normal age of confirmation was fixed at seven years old, but the practice of confirming younger infants when a bishop was available persisted throughout the Middle Ages. For example, in 1533, the future Queen Elizabeth I was baptised and confirmed when she was only three days old, because a bishop was readily available at the royal court.

During the Middle Ages, there was a continuing debate about the relationship between the three sacraments of baptism, confirmation and Holy Communion. It was accepted, in line with Christian practice from the earliest times, that baptism had to precede admission to Holy Communion, but there was discussion about whether confirmation had to precede Holy Communion as well. In England, Archbishop John Peckham decreed at the Council of Lambeth in 1281 that no-one should be admitted to Communion before he or she was confirmed. This regulation seems to have been aimed at bolstering confirmation by giving people an incentive to have their children confirmed. In line with this regulation, the rubric of the Manual of the Sarum Rite declared that 'no one must be admitted to the sacrament of the body and blood of Christ save in danger of death, unless he has been confirmed or has been reasonably prevented from receiving the sacrament of confirmation'.[8]

---

[8] Cameron, 'Development of Confirmation,' 74.

Conclusion

What we have seen in this chapter is that there was a clear understanding and practice of Christian initiation in the Western Church by the end of the Middle Ages, which was a development of the understanding and practice of initiation that existed the Church of the Patristic period.

The understanding was that there were two sacraments of Christian initiation: baptism and confirmation. Through the baptism, Christians received new life in Christ and the remission of their sins through the Spirit. Through confirmation, they received additional strength to live for Christ and to do battle with the forces of evil through the Spirit.

The practice was for children to be baptised by a priest very soon after birth and for those same children to be confirmed at a later age by a bishop, with the matter of the confirmation rite being the bishop anointing the candidates with the oil of chrism.

At the Reformation, the leaders of the Church of England in the sixteenth and seventeenth centuries reassessed the understanding and practice of the English Medieval church's understanding of the teaching and practice of Scripture and the Fathers. This reassessment led them to reject some aspects of the Medieval pattern of Christian initiation while retaining others.

As we shall see in the next chapter, the confirmation service in the *Book of Common Prayer* is the result of this process of rejection and retention.

Chapter 2:

The development of the confirmation service in the *Book of Common Prayer*

In chapter 1 we looked at the emergence and development of the rite of confirmation in the Patristic and Medieval periods. In this chapter we shall go on to look at how the Church of England's service of confirmation in the *Book of Common Prayer* developed over the course of the sixteenth and seventeenth centuries and the theological reasons for this development.

The *Sarum Rite*

A good place to start when tracing the development of the confirmation service in the *Book of Common Prayer* is with the confirmation service in the *Sarum Rite*. This confirmation rite, the text of which was in Latin, was not the only one used in England at the end of the Middle Ages. However, as E C Whitaker and Maxwell Johnson explain, it was:

> ...the initiatory rite which was in use in many parts of England on the eve of the Reformation, and it reflects the pastoral situation which Cranmer and his colleagues had known all their lives when they addressed themselves to the task of revising the offices of baptism and confirmation.[1]

---

[1] Whitaker and Johnson, *Documents of the Baptismal Liturgy*, 284.

In English translation the *Sarum Rite* confirmation service runs as follows:

The Confirmation of Children

First let the bishop say:

Our Help.

Let the name of the Lord etc.

The Lord be with you.

And with your spirit.

Let us pray

Almighty and everlasting God who has deigned to regenerate these your servants (or these your handmaids) by water and the Holy Spirit, and has given unto them the remission of all their sins, send upon them the sevenfold Holy Spirit, the Paraclete from heaven. Amen.

The Spirit of wisdom and understanding. Amen.

The Spirit of knowledge and piety. Amen.

The Spirit of counsel and fortitude + Amen.

And fill them with the Spirit of the fear of the Lord. Amen.

And sign them with the sign of the holy cross + and confirm them with the chrism of salvation unto life eternal. Amen.

And then let the bishop ask the name and anoint his thumb with chrism: and let him make on the forehead of the child a cross saying:

I sign you N. with the sign of the cross + and I confirm you with the chrism of salvation, in the name of the Father + and of the Son + and of the Holy Spirit. + Amen.

Peace be to you.

Let us pray:

Prayer

God who to your apostles gave the Holy Spirit and who wished him to be given through them to their successors and to the rest of the faithful people, look mercifully upon our humble family, and grant that the hearts of those whose foreheads we have anointed with holy chrism and signed with the sign of the holy cross the same Holy Spirit may come and make into a temple of his glory by deigning to dwell therein. Through our Lord. In the unity of the same.

Behold, thus shall be blessed every man who fears the Lord.

The Lord bless you out of Sion, that you may see the good things of Jerusalem all your days.

Almighty God bless you, the Father + and the Son + and the Holy Spirit. + Amen.[1]

This service stands in the liturgical tradition of the *Galesian Sacramentary*. It is a service with two main foci. First, there is a prayer for the gift of the sevenfold Spirit and second there is the liturgical action by the bishop which takes the form of the bishop using chrism to sign those being confirmed with the sign of the cross.

In some confirmation rites the bishop also gave the person being confirmed 'a light blow to the side of the face to remind him that he must be ready to fight manfully as "goddes champion".'[2]

The confirmation service in the 1549 Prayer Book

The first confirmation service produced by the English Reformers after the break with Rome was that contained in the 1549 Prayer Book. It ran as follows:[3]

---

[1] Text in Whitaker and Johnson, *Documents of the Baptismal Liturgy*, 306–07. Where there is a cross in the text this is a sign that the bishop should make the sign of the cross.
[2] Frank Colquhoun, *The Catechism and the Order of Confirmation* (London: Hodder and Stoughton, 1963), 168.
[3] The text is from http://justus.anglican.org/resources/bcp/1549/Confirmation_1549.htm with the spelling updated.

CONFIRMATION.

Our help is in the name of the Lord.
Answer. Which hath made both heaven and earth.
Minister. Blessed is the name of the lord.
Answer. Henceforth world without end.
Minister. The lord be with you.
Answer. And with thy spirit.

Let us pray.

ALMIGHTY and ever-living God, who hast vouchsafed to regenerate these thy servants of water and the Holy Ghost: And hast given unto them forgiveness of all their sins: Send down from heaven we beseech thee, (O lord) upon them thy Holy Ghost the comforter, with the manifold gifts of grace, the spirit of wisdom and understanding; the spirit of counsel and ghostly strength; The spirit of knowledge and true godliness, and fulfil them, (O lord) with the spirit of thy holy fear.

Answer. Amen.

Minister. Sign them (O lord) and mark them to be thine for ever, by the virtue of thy holy cross and passion. Confirm and strengthen them with the inward unction of thy Holy Ghost, mercifully unto everlasting life. Amen.

Then the Bishop shall cross them in the forehead, and lay his hands upon their heads, saying

N. I sign thee with the sign of the cross, and lay my hand upon thee. In the name of the Father, and of the Son, and of the Holy Ghost. Amen.

And thus shall he do to every child one after another. And when he hath laid his hand upon every child, then shall he say.

The peace of the lord abide with you. *Answer.* And with thy spirit.

¶ Let us pray.

ALMIGHTY ever-living God, which makest us both to will and to do those things that be good and acceptable unto thy majesty: we make our humble supplications unto thee for these children, upon whom (after the example of thy holy apostles) we have laid our hands, to certify them (by this sign) of thy favour and gracious goodness toward them: let thy fatherly hand (we beseech thee) ever be over them, let thy Holy Spirit ever be with them, and so lead them in the knowledge and obedience of thy word, that in the end they may obtain the life everlasting, through our lord Jesus Christ, who with thee and the Holy Ghost liveth and reigneth one God world without end. Amen.

Then shall the Bishop bless the children, thus saying.

The blessing of God almighty, the Father, the Son, and the Holy Ghost, be upon you, and remain with you forever. Amen.

The curate of every parish once in six weeks at the least upon warning by him given, shall upon some Sunday or holy day, half an hour before evensong openly in the church instruct and examine so many children of his parish sent unto him, as the time will serve, and as he shall think convenient, in some part of this Catechism. And all fathers, mothers, masters, and dames, shall cause their children, servants, and apprentices (which are not yet confirmed), to come to the church at the day appointed, and obediently hear and be ordered by the curate, until such time as they have learned all that is here appointed for them to learn.

¶ And when so ever the Bishop shall give knowledge for children to be brought afore him to any convenient place, for their confirmation: Then shall the curate of every parish either bring or send in writing, ye names of all those children of his parish which can say the articles of their faith, the Lord's Prayer, and the Ten Commandments. And also how many of

them can answer to the other questions contained in this Catechism.

¶ And there shall none be admitted to the Holy Communion: until such time as he be confirmed.

There are four key differences between this service and the confirmation service in the *Sarum Rite:*

1. Unlike the *Sarum Rite*, the 1549 confirmation rite (like its successors in 1552 and 1662) is in English rather than Latin.

2. Unlike the *Sarum Rite*, which makes no provision for the instruction of those who are to be confirmed, the 1549 rite included a catechism preceding the confirmation service itself. This catechism (omitted here for reasons of space) was probably written by future Dean of St. Paul's, Alexander Nowell.[4] It reminded children of the promises made for them by their godparents at their baptism and instruction on the Apostles' Creed, the Ten Commandments and the Lord's Prayer. This catechism is the catechism referred to in the rubrics at the end of the service which explain how religious instruction should be given by the parochial clergy to children and young people on the basis of the material which it contains.

3. Although in the 1549 rite the bishop makes the sign of the cross on the forehead of the person being confirmed, there is no anointing with oil (or buffeting

---

[4] For the evidence, see Martin Davie, *Instruction in the Way of the Lord* (London: Latimer Trust, 2014), 15-17.

the side of the head) and the bishop lays his hand upon them.

4. After the act of confirmation itself there is a collect derived from the confirmation service written by Archbishop Hermann of Cologne. In this collect, confirmation is seen in terms of the laying on of hands 'after the example of thy holy apostles', emphasising that it is the laying on of the bishop's hand that is at the centre of the rite and tracing the biblical origins of confirmation back to Acts 8 and Acts 19.

The Confirmation service in the 1552 Prayer Book

As in the case of the 1549 Prayer Book as a whole, the 1549 confirmation rite was reissued in a revised form in 1552. The revised rite runs as follows, with changes from the 1549 text in bold.[5] As in the case of the 1549 rite, the 1552 rite begins with the text of the catechism, which has been omitted here for reasons of space.

CONFIRMATION.

Our help is in the name of the Lord.
Answer. Which hath made both heaven and earth.
Minister. Blessed is the name of the Lord.
Answer. Henceforth world without end.
Minister. Lord hear our prayer.
Answer. And let out cry come to thee.

---

[5] The text is from http://justus.anglican.org/resources/bcp/1552/Confirmation_1552.htm with the spelling updated.

Let us pray.

ALMIGHTY and ever-living God, who hast vouchsafed to regenerate these thy servants by water and the Holy Ghost, and hast given unto them forgiveness of all their sins: strengthen them, we beseech thee, (O Lord,) with the Holy Ghost the comforter, and daily increase in them thy manifold gifts of grace, the spirit of wisdom and understanding; the spirit of counsel and ghostly strength, the spirit of knowledge and true godliness: and fulfil them, (O lord,) with the spirit of thy holy fear. Amen.

Then the Bishop shall lay his hand upon every child severally, saying,

DEFEND, O lord, this child with thy heavenly grace, that he may continue thine for ever, and daily increase in thy Holy Spirit more and more, until he come unto thy everlasting kingdom. Amen.

Then shall the Bishop say.

¶ Let us pray.

ALMIGHTY ever-living God, which makest us both to will and to do those things that be good and acceptable unto thy Majesty: we make our humble supplications unto thee for these children, upon whom (after the example of thy holy Apostles) we have laid our hands, to certify them (by this sign) of thy favour and gracious goodness toward them: let thy fatherly hand (we beseech thee) ever be over them, let thy Holy Spirit ever be with them, and so lead them in the knowledge and obedience of thy word, that in the end they may obtain the everlasting life, through our Lord Jesus Christ, who with thee and the Holy Ghost liveth and reigneth one God, world without end. Amen

Then the Bishop shall bless the children, thus saying.

THE blessing of God Almighty, the Father, the Son, and the Holy Ghost, be upon you, and remain with you for ever. Amen.

The Curate of every Parish, or some other at his appointment, shall diligently upon Sundays, and holy days half an hour before Evensong, openly in the Church instruct and examine so many children of his parish sent unto him, as the time will serve, and as he shall think convenient, in some part of this Catechism

And all Fathers, Mothers, Masters, and Dames. shall cause their children, servants, and apprentices (which have not learned their Catechism), to come to the church at the time appointed, and obediently to hear and be ordered by the Curate, until such time as they have learned all that is here

> *appointed for them to learn. And whensoever the Bishop shall give knowledge for children to be brought afore him to any convenient place, for their confirmation: then shall the Curate of every parish either bring, or send in writing, the names of all those children of his parish which can say the Articles of their faith, the Lord's Prayer, and the x Commandments: and also how many of them can answer to the other questions contained in this Catechism.*
>
> *And there shall none be admitted to the Holy Communion, until such time as he can say the Catechism, and be confirmed.*

The key changes in the 1552 rite are as follows:

1. The versicles and responses at the beginning of the service now end with a plea addressed to God to hear the prayers which will be offered in the rest of the service.

2. The prayer before the act of confirmation by the bishop is now a prayer, not for God to 'send down' the Holy Spirit on the candidates (which might imply that they had not received the Spirit when they were baptised), but for him to 'strengthen' them by the Spirit and 'daily increase' in them the sevenfold gifts of the Spirit.

3. The signing with the cross has vanished and the act of confirmation takes place solely through the laying on of the bishop's hand.

4. There is a new prayer accompanying the act of confirmation which asks God to 'defend' those who have been confirmed from forces of evil and, as before, also asks that they will 'daily increase in thy Holy Spirit'.

5. In the final rubric, admission to Communion is restricted not only to those who have been confirmed, as in the Medieval tradition, but to those who can recite the catechism as well.

The confirmation service in the 1662 Prayer Book

Further changes were made to the confirmation service as part of the general revision of the Prayer Book after the restoration of the monarchy in 1660. The 1662 service which is the *Book of Common Prayer* confirmation service still in use today is as follows (with changes from the 1552 rite in bold):[6]

> **THE ORDER OF CONFIRMATION; or Laying on of Hands upon those that are baptized and come to years of discretion**
>
> *Upon the day appointed, all that are to be then confirmed, being placed, and standing in order before the Bishop; he (or some other Minister appointed by him) shall read this Preface following.*
>
> **TO the end that Confirmation may be ministered to the more edifying of such as shall receive it, the Church hath thought good to order, That none hereafter shall be**

---

6 http://justus.anglican.org/resources/bcp/1662/catechism&conf.pdf

confirmed, but such as can say the Creed, the Lord's Prayer, and the Ten Commandments; and can also answer to such other Questions, as in the short Catechism are contained: which order is very convenient to be observed; to the end that children being now come to the years of discretion, and having learned what their Godfathers and Godmothers promised for them in Baptism, they may themselves, with their own mouth and consent, openly before the Church, ratify and confirm the same; and also promise, that by the grace of God they will evermore endeavour themselves faithfully to observe such things, as they by their own confession have assented unto.

Then shall the Bishop say,

DO ye here, in the presence of God, and of this Congregation, renew the solemn promise and vow that was made in your name at your Baptism; ratifying and confirming the same in your own persons, and acknowledging yourselves bound to believe and to do all those things, which your Godfathers and Godmothers then undertook for you?

And every one shall audibly answer,

I do.

The Bishop. Our help is in the Name of the Lord;
Answer. Who hath made heaven and earth.
Bishop. Blessed be the Name of the Lord;
Answer. Henceforth world without end.
Bishop. Lord, hear our prayers;
Answer. And let our cry come unto thee.

Bishop. Let us pray.

ALMIGHTY and ever-living God, who hast vouchsafed to regenerate these thy servants by Water and the Holy Ghost, and hast given unto them forgiveness of all their sins: Strengthen them, we beseech thee, O Lord, with the Holy Ghost the Comforter, and daily increase in them thy manifold gifts of grace; the spirit of wisdom and understanding; the spirit of counsel and ghostly strength; the spirit of knowledge and true godliness; and fill them, O Lord, with the spirit of thy holy fear, now and for ever. **Amen.**

Then all of them in order kneeling before the Bishop, he shall lay his hand upon the head of every one severally, saying,

DEFEND, O Lord, this thy Child **[or *this thy Servant*]** with thy heavenly grace, that *he* may continue thine for ever; and daily increase in thy Holy Spirit, more and more, until *he* come unto thy everlasting kingdom. *Amen.*

Then shall the Bishop say,

Bishop. The Lord be with you.
Answer. And with thy spirit.

And (all kneeling down) the Bishop shall add,
Let us pray.

OUR Father which art in heaven, Hallowed be thy Name, Thy kingdom come, Thy will be done, in earth as it is in heaven. Give us this day our daily bread; And forgive us our trespasses, As we forgive them that trespass against us; And lead us not into temptation, But deliver us from evil. Amen.

And this Collect.

ALMIGHTY and ever-living God, who makest us both to will and to do those things that be good and acceptable unto thy divine Majesty; We make our humble supplications unto thee for these thy servants, upon whom, after the example of thy holy Apostles, we have now laid our hands, to certify them (by this sign) of thy favour and gracious goodness towards them. Let thy fatherly hand, we beseech thee, ever be over them; let thy Holy Spirit ever be with them; and so lead them in the knowledge and obedience of thy Word, that in the end they may obtain everlasting life; through our Lord Jesus Christ, who with thee and the Holy Ghost liveth and reigneth, ever one God, world without end. **Amen.**

O ALMIGHTY Lord, and everlasting God, vouchsafe, we beseech thee, to direct, sanctify, and govern both our hearts and bodies, in the ways of thy laws, and in the works of thy commandments; that through thy most mighty protection, both here and ever, we may be preserved in body and soul; through our Lord and Saviour Jesus Christ. **Amen.**

Then the Bishop shall bless them, saying thus,

THE blessing of God Almighty, the Father, the Son, and the Holy Ghost, be upon you, and remain with you, for ever. **Amen.**

And there shall none be admitted to the holy Communion, until such time as he be confirmed, ***or be ready and desirous to be confirmed.***

The key changes to the 1552 rite in the 1662 service are as follows:

1. The catechism, which had been extended in 1604 to include material on the sacraments, was taken out of the confirmation service itself and given its own place in the *Book of Common Prayer* between the baptism services and the confirmation service.

2. The confirmation service starts with a new preface, which draws on the rubrics at the start of the 1549 and 1552 rites and which sets out the Church of England's requirements for confirmation.

3. There then follows a renewal by the candidates for baptism of the promise that was made by their godparents when they were baptised. This material is drawn from the work of Archbishop Herman of Cologne.

4. It is specified that that those who are to be confirmed will kneel and that the bishop will lay his hand on the head of each of them 'severally' – that is, 'individually'.

5. The use of the word 'servant' is specified as an alternative to 'child' to be used in the case of adult candidates.

6. After the act of confirmation, the Lord's Prayer is added as an introduction to the final prayers.

7. An additional collect is added for the preservation of the faithful in their bodies and souls. This collect is one of the occasional prayers at the end of the Prayer Book Communion service and comes from a seventh-century work called the *Sacramentary of Gregory*.

8. In the final rubric the requirement to be able to recite the catechism is omitted and it is stipulated that those who are 'ready and desirous to be confirmed' may be admitted to Communion as well as those who have actually been confirmed. This final change reflected the fact that people had not had access to bishops in order to be confirmed during the period of the Civil War and the Commonwealth.

What understanding of confirmation underlies these developments?

In the first part of this chapter, we have looked at the developments that took place in the Church of England's confirmation service during the course of the sixteenth and seventeenth centuries. Now we shall go on to look at the understanding of confirmation that lies behind these developments.

We shall draw on two sources of information: the rubrics at the beginning of the 1552 Prayer Book and statements by individual Church of England theologians.

The rubrics in the 1552 Prayer Book, which are a light edited version of those in the 1549 Prayer Book, run as follows:

> To the end that Confirmation may be ministered to the more edifying of such as shall receive it (according unto saint Paul's doctrine, who teaches that all things should be done in the Church to the edification of the same) it is thought good that none hereafter shall be confirmed, but such as can say in their mother tongue the articles of the faith, the Lord's Prayer, and the x commandments; And can also answer to such questions of this short Catechism, as the Bishop (or such as he shall appoint) shall by his discretion appose[7] them in. And this order is most convenient to be observed for divers considerations.

---

[7] Examine.

First, because that when children come to the years of discretion, and have learned what their godfathers and godmothers promised for them in baptism, they may then themselves with their own mouth, and with their own consent, openly before the Church, ratify and confirm the same: and also promise that by the grace of God they will evermore endeavour themselves faithfully to observe and keep such things, as they by their own mouth and confession have assented unto.

Secondly, for as much as Confirmation is ministered to them that be Baptized, that by imposition of hands and Prayer they may receive strength and defence against all temptations to sin and the assaults of the world, and the Devil: it is most mete to be ministered when children come to that age, that partly by the frailty of their own flesh, partly by the assaults of the world and the Devil, they begin to be in danger to fall into sundry kinds of sin.

Thirdly, for that it is agreeable with the usage of the Church in times past, whereby it was ordained that Confirmation should be ministered to them that were of perfect age[8], that they being instructed in Christ's religion, should openly Profess their own

---

[8] In other words, adults.

> faith, and promise to be obedient unto the will of God.
>
> And that no man shall think that any detriment shall come to children by deferring of their Confirmation; he shall know for truth, that it is certain by God's word, that children being baptized, have all things necessary for their salvation, and be undoubtedly saved.

The rubrics begin by declaring that Paul's principle 'let all things be done for edification' (1 Cor 14:26) is what underlies the requirement that those who are confirmed must be able both to recite the Apostles Creed, the Lord's Prayer and the Ten Commandments and also be able to answer the questions contained in the catechism about their meaning.

This requirement is said to be 'convenient' (in other words, fitting or appropriate) for three reasons:

First, insisting on this requirement creates the opportunity for those who have been baptised as infants to own for themselves what was promised for them at their baptism and to promise that with God's help they will endeavour to faithfully live it out.

This point was important for the English Reformers because it enabled them to make sense of the practice of infant baptism.

We can see this in the *Larger Catechism* of Alexander Nowell. In this work, the teacher or 'master' (M) asks his pupil or 'scholar' (S) why it is appropriate to baptise infants when they can neither confess the faith nor repent of their sins (both of which are necessary for baptism):

> M. Sith[9] infants cannot by age perform those things that thou speakest of, why are they baptized?

The answer given by the pupil is as follows:

> S. That faith and repentance go before baptism, is required only in persons so grown in years, that by age they are capable of both. But to infants the promise made to the Church by Christ, in whose faith they are baptized, shall for the present time be sufficient; and then afterward, when they are grown to years, they must needs themselves acknowledge the truth of their baptism, and have the force thereof to be lively in their souls, and to be represented in their life and behaviours.[10]

For the English Reformers a key part of the importance of confirmation was that it gave the opportunity for those baptised in infancy to 'acknowledge the truth of their baptism' and to represent it in 'their life and behaviours' by publicly turning away from sin and turning to the path of Christian obedience.

Secondly, through prayer and the laying of hands, those who are confirmed have the opportunity to receive strength from God through the Spirit to battle successfully against temptations to sin arising internally from their own fallen nature inherited from Adam and, externally, from the world

---

[9] 'Sith' here means 'since'.
[10] G. E. Corrie, ed., *Nowell's Catechism* (Cambridge: Parker Society/CUP, 1843), 209.

and the Devil.[11] This temptation grows as people move from infancy towards adulthood and so it is pastorally appropriate and important for people to be confirmed at this point in their lives at a point where the (relative) innocence of childhood has not yet changed into a fixed pattern of sin.

This idea of receiving strength and defence against the assaults of the flesh, the world and the devil, builds on the understanding of the purpose of confirmation which we saw in the previous chapter in the Pentecost sermon from Faustus of Riez. As we shall see in more detail in the next chapter, this view of the purpose of confirmation has its roots in the teaching of the New Testament and is an integral part of the theology of the confirmation service.

Thirdly, the requirement that candidates for confirmation should receive instruction and be able and willing to make a profession of their faith and of their commitment to living the Christian life is in line with practice of the Early Church. During that time, those who received the laying on of hands from the bishop after baptism were those who had received catechetical instruction and who made profession of their faith and their commitment to live as Christians.[12]

The English Reformers, like their continental counterparts, believed that in the Early Church those baptised as infants were catechized before being brought to a bishop for confirmation. Nowell, for instance, writes:

---

[11] On inheriting our fallen nature from Adam, see Article IX 'Of Original or Birth Sin.'
[12] A good example of the form that catechetical instruction took in the Early Church can be found in the fourth-century *Catechetical Lectures* of Cyril of Jerusalem, which can be found in *The Nicene and Post-Nicene Fathers*, second series, vol. vii.

S. Parents and schoolmasters did in old time diligently instruct their children, as soon as by age they were able to perceive and understand, in the first principles of Christian religion, that they might suck in godliness almost together with the nurse's milk, and straightways after their cradle might be nourished with the tender food of virtue towards that blessed life. For the which purpose also little short books, which we name Catechisms, were written, wherein the same, or very like matters as we now are in hand with, were entreated upon. And after that the children seemed to be sufficiently trained in the principles of our religion, they brought and offered them unto the bishop.

M. For what purpose did they so?
S. That children might after baptism do the same which such as were older, who were also called *catechumeni,* that is, scholars of religion, did in old time before, or rather, at baptism itself. For the bishop did require and the children did render reason and account of their religion and faith: and such children as the bishop judged to have sufficiently profited in the understanding of religion he allowed, and laying his hands upon them, and blessing them, let them

depart. This allowance and blessing of the bishop our men do call Confirmation.[13]

Patristic scholars today are doubtful whether the catechesis of baptised infants followed by confirmation was practised in the Early Church, but where the Reformers were right was in seeing catechesis as a central part of the process of Christian initiation in the Early Church and as being something that preceded the laying on hands by the bishop.

The requirement that those to be confirmed should have received instruction and should be capable of confessing the faith for themselves necessarily ruled out the Medieval practice of confirming children in early infancy.

This change in the age at which people were confirmed caused parents anxiety because although the Church's official teaching was that confirmation was not necessary for salvation, as we have noted, it was popularly held that there were two parts to becoming a Christian and thus being saved – baptism and confirmation. This meant that children who died before confirmation were in danger of forfeiting their salvation. The final rubric in the 1552 rite addresses this anxiety by assuring anxious parents on the authority of 'God's word' that 'that children, being baptised, have all things necessary for their salvation, and be undoubtedly saved.'

The justification for this claim is not given in the confirmation service itself, but it can be found in the services for the baptism of infants in the Prayer Book. In these services the priest reads the account of Jesus welcoming and blessing infants in Mark 10:13–16.

---

[13] Corrie, *Nowell's Catechism*, 210–211.

The priest then explains to the congregation why this reading shows that Jesus will bestow eternal life on the infant who has been brought for baptism and after this explanation he prays for the child on the basis of what he has just said:

> Beloved, ye hear in this Gospel the words of our Saviour Christ, that he commanded the children to be brought unto him; how he blamed those that would have kept them from him; how he exhorteth all men to follow their innocency. Ye perceive how by his outward gesture and deed he declared his good will toward them; for he embraced them in his arms, he laid his hands upon them, and blessed them. Doubt ye not therefore, but earnestly believe, that he will likewise favourably receive this present Infant; that he will embrace him with the arms of his mercy; that he will give unto him the blessing of eternal life, and make him partaker of his everlasting kingdom. Wherefore we being thus persuaded of the good will of our heavenly Father towards this Infant, declared by his Son Jesus Christ; and nothing doubting but that he favourably alloweth this charitable work of ours in bringing this Infant to his holy Baptism; let us faithfully and devoutly give thanks unto him, and say,
>
> Almighty and everlasting God, heavenly Father, we give thee humble thanks that thou hast vouchsafed to call us to the

knowledge of thy grace and faith in thee: Increase this knowledge, and confirm this faith in us evermore. Give thy Holy Spirit to this Infant, that he may be born again, and be made an heir of everlasting salvation, through our Lord Jesus Christ, who liveth and reigneth with thee and the Holy Spirit, now and for ever. Amen.[14]

It was because the Reformers believed the theology set out in the baptism service that they were confident about the salvation of baptised infants and felt that confirmation could be delayed without putting the salvation of young children in peril.

Not only did the English Reformers reject the practice of confirming infants, but they also rejected two other aspects of Medieval understanding and practice with regard to confirmation as well.

First, they denied that confirmation was a sacrament. In the words of Article XXV, they held that: 'There are two Sacraments ordained of Christ our Lord in the Gospel, that is to say, Baptism and the Supper of the Lord.' In consequence, the article says: 'Those five commonly called Sacraments, that is to say, Confirmation, Penance, Orders, Matrimony and Extreme Unction, are not to be counted for Sacraments of the Gospel.'

The reason why the English Reformers held that confirmation was not a sacrament is explained by John Jewel in his work *A Treatise of the Sacraments*. He argues that although confirmation is 'profitable' and 'necessary' when rightly used

---

[14] *The Book of Common Prayer,* the services for the 'Publick Baptism of Infants' and the 'Private Baptism of Infants'.

(for the reasons we have noted above) this does not mean it is a sacrament. It lacks an essential element of a sacrament, namely being a ceremony instituted by Christ himself:

> Now, whether it be a sacrament: and when I say a Sacrament, I mean a ceremony commanded by God in express words. For God only hath the authority to institute a sacrament. Sacraments are confirmations and seals of the promises of God, and are not of the earth, but from heaven. As Christ saith: 'The baptism of John, whence was it? from heaven or of men?' Chrysostom saith, the mystery were not of God, nor perfect, if thou shouldest put anything to it. Mark, and judge, and yourselves shall see, whether this were a sacrament instituted by Christ. Augustine said: *Accedat verbum ad elementum, & fit sacramentum*: 'Join the word to the creature, and it is made a sacrament.' This creature or element is visible, as are water, bread and wine. The word which must be joined, is the commandment and institution of Christ: without the word, and the commandment and institution, it is no sacrament.
>
> I protest, that the use and order of confirmation rightly used is profitable, and necessary in the Church, and no way to be broken. But all that is profitable and necessary is not a sacrament. Christ did not command it; he spake no word of it. Look

> and read if you doubt it; Christ's words are written, and may be seen. You shall never find that he commanded Confirmation or that he ever made any special promise to it. Therefore may you conclude, that it is no sacrament. Otherwise, being rightly used, it is a good ceremony, and well ordained of our ancient fathers.[15]

Secondly, as is made clear by the changes between the confirmation service in the *Sarum Rite* and the subsequent Church of England confirmation services, the English Reformers rejected the use of the oil of chrism in the confirmation service. As we have previously noted, in Medieval thinking the use of the oil of chrism tended to be regarded as the essential 'matter' of the confirmation service, but the English Reformers did away with it completely.

The reason they did so is again explained by Jewel in the treatise just mentioned. Jewel declares that when it came to confirmation, the misuse of oil meant that there was 'great abuse in the manner of doing' in the Medieval Church:

> For thus the bishop said: *Consigno te signo crucis*, & *confirmo te chrismate salutis:* 'I sign thee with the sign of the cross, and confirm thee with the oil of salvation.' Thus they used to do, these were their words: 'with the oil of salvation.' They took not this of Christ, nor of his Apostles, nor of the holy

---

[15] John Jewel, *A Treatise of the Sacraments* in John Ayre, ed., *The Works of John Jewel: The Second Portion* (Cambridge: Parker Society/CUP, 1848), 1125–26.

ancient Fathers. It agreeth not with our Christian faith to give the power of salvation unto oil. He that seeketh salvation in oil, loseth his salvation in Christ, and hath no part in the kingdom of God. Oil is for the belly, and for necessary uses of life. It is no fit instrument, without commandment or promise by the word, to work salvation.[16]

Developing further his criticism of the way in which the Medieval Church attributed saying power to the oil, he notes that this led to an undervaluing of the significance of baptism:

...they said he was no perfect Christian that was not anointed by the bishop with this holy oil. This was another abuse. For whosoever is baptized receiveth thereby the full name of a perfect Christian, and hath the full and perfect covenant and assurance of salvation: he is perfectly buried with Christ; doth perfectly put on Christ, and is perfectly made partaker of his resurrection. Therefore they are deceived, that say, no man is a perfect Christian that is not marked with this oil. Else the Apostles, and holy Martyrs were but half Christians, because they lacked this oil. Else, what hope and comfort might the poor Fathers have? In what state shall he think to find his child, if he die before confirmation, and pass without perfect Christendom? Verily they

---

[16] Ayre, *Works of John Jewel*, 1126.

write thus: *Sine oleo chrismatis nemo potest sisti ante tribunal Christi*: 'Without the oil of Chrism, no man can appear before the judgment seat of Christ.'[17]

In addition, he writes, it led to the oil being credited with the saving power that properly belongs to the death of Christ:

> ...when they blessed or hallowed their oil, they used these words: *Fiat, Domine, hoc oleum, te benedicente, unctio spiritualis ad purificationem mentis et corporis*: 'O Lord, let this oil, by thy blessing, be made a spiritual ointment, to purify both soul and body.' O Christ Jesu, where was thy cross, where was thy blood, and the price of thy death and passion, when a drop of oil was of power to work remission of all sins, to save and defend against all the darts of the wicked spirits, and to refresh both body and soul? Yet so were we taught, so were we led. I feign not these things: the words may be seen. Neither do I speak this to bring you to a misliking or loathing of our late fathers: but only that we may humble our hearts, and give thanks to God that hath brought us out of that darkness, and given us better knowledge.[18]

---

[17] Ayre, *Works of John Jewel*, 1126.
[18] Ayre, *Works of John Jewel*, 1126.

In place of the use of oil, the Reformers went back instead to the biblical and early Patristic model of the laying on of hands with prayer.

In his chapter, we have traced the development of the confirmation service in the *Book of Common Prayer* during the course of the sixteenth and seventeen centuries. We have noted the changes that took place in the confirmation service between the *Sarum Rite* and the 1662 rite and have explored the reasons why these changes were made.

In the next chapter we shall go on to look at the 1662 service in more detail.

CHAPTER 3:

A COMMENTARY ON THE CONFIRMATION SERVICE IN THE *BOOK OF COMMON PRAYER*

In this chapter we shall set out the overall shape of the 1662 confirmation service and then work through it section by section, looking at what it says in detail.

The overall shape of the 1662 service

The 1662 service can be usefully divided into three main parts.

- The first part consists of the preface which explains the qualifications for confirmation and a renewal by the confirmation candidates of the 'promise and vow' made on their behalf at their baptism.

- The second part consists of prayer for the sevenfold gifts of the Spirit followed by prayer and the laying on the hand by the bishop.

- The third part consists of further prayers both for the candidates and for all those present.

The service concludes with a blessing by the bishop.

As Frank Colquhoun notes, there are 'two distinct actions in the service.'[1]

First, he writes:

> ...the candidates, presenting themselves before God as those who have been baptized into the Church of Christ, publicly ratify their vows and in so doing make good that

---
[1] Colquhoun, *Catechism and Confirmation*, 172.

element of personal faith which had been lacking before. For this purpose they *stand*.[2]

Next, he says:

> ...comes the confirmation proper, in which we turn from the human to the divine side of the action. Here we look to God to do his part: to sanctify and strengthen his children that they may be able to live up to their profession. Hence the candidates now *kneel* before the bishop and seek the blessing of God's Holy Spirit through the laying on of hands.[3]

What Colquhoun fails to note, but which is also important, is that after the laying on of hands the candidates and congregation all kneel while prayers are led by the bishop asking God to continue and complete his work of grace, both in the life of those who have just been confirmed, and in the lives of everyone else who is present.

When looked at in this way it becomes clear that the bulk of the confirmation service is taken up with prayer. The candidates renew the promises made for them at their confirmation, they then acknowledge that they (like the rest of God's people) need God's help to keep these promises, and the rest of the service consists of prayer asking God to give this help.

We will now consider each section in turn.

---

[2] Colquhoun, *Catechism and Confirmation*, 172. Italics in the original.
[3] Colquhoun, *Catechism and Confirmation*, 172. Italics in the original.

The title for the service

> THE ORDER OF CONFIRMATION; or Laying on of Hands upon those that are baptized and come to years of discretion.

The title of the service raises the question of the meaning of the term 'confirmation'. What is not often understood is that in the 1662 service, 'confirm' and 'confirmation' are used in two different ways.

In the preface to the service 'confirm' is used as a synonym for 'ratify' when it is said that that candidates have the opportunity to 'ratify and confirm' what their 'Godfathers and Godmothers promised for them in Baptism.'

However, in the title of the service and in the opening line of the preface 'confirmation' is used in a different sense. The Latin word *confirmare* from which the English words 'confirm' and 'confirmation' are derived means 'strengthen' and in the title and the first line of the preface 'confirmation' (as in the work of Faustus of Riez) refers to the strengthening (or 'confirmation') of the candidates by God in response to prayer.

In the 1662 service, the words 'ratify and confirm' replace the words 'ratify and confess' in the original 1549 service. The result of this change has been confusion between the two different meanings of confirm and confirmation as it has led to people seeking to understand the service as if the words had a single meaning. Thus, it has sometimes been said that in the confirmation service the candidates confirm their faith in God and that God confirms their status as Christian people. This is a misunderstanding of the service.

In the first part of the service, the confirmation candidates do indeed confirm (in the sense of 'ratify') their faith, but nothing is said in the service about God confirming their status as Christians. As we have seen, the rest of the service after the ratification of the baptismal promises consists of prayer asking God to confirm (in the sense of 'make firm' or 'strengthen') the candidates for the rest of their Christian life and ministry. Jesus was strengthened by the Spirit after his baptism in the Jordan. The apostles were strengthened by the Spirit at Pentecost. Now God is asked to strengthen those who have ratified their baptismal promises.

The reason why in the title of the service the words 'confirmation or laying on of hands' are used is because, as we shall see below, the laying on of the bishop's hand is the sign that prayer is being offered to God for this purpose.

The opening rubric and the preface

Upon the day appointed, all that are to be then confirmed, being placed, and standing in order before the Bishop; he (or some other Minister appointed by him) shall read this Preface following.

TO the end that Confirmation may be ministered to the more edifying of such as shall receive it, the Church hath thought good to order, That none hereafter shall be confirmed, but such as can say the Creed, the Lord's Prayer, and the Ten Commandments; and can also answer to such other Questions, as in the short Catechism are contained: which order is very convenient to be observed; to the end that children being now come to the years of discretion, and having learned what their Godfathers and Godmothers promised for them in Baptism, they may themselves, with their own mouth and consent, openly before the Church, ratify and confirm the same; and also promise, that by the grace of God they will evermore endeavour themselves faithfully to observe such things, as they by their own confession have assented unto.

The opening rubric gives the necessary instructions for the start of the service. As noted above, in the confirmation service candidates stand to confess their faith and the reason they are already standing here is because they are shortly going to confess their faith.

The words of the preface are spoken either by the bishop, or by some other minister appointed by him for this task. They explain that in line with Paul's injunction in 1 Corinthians 14:26 that what is done in church services should be for the purpose of 'edification' (in other words, the spiritual improvement) of those present. The Church of England has laid down that in order to be confirmed a person has to be able to say the Creed (in other words, the Apostles Creed), the Lord's Prayer and the Ten Commandments, and also answer the questions about them, about the baptismal promises, and about the sacraments, which are contained in the Prayer Book catechism.[4]

---

[4] The reason that reference is made to the 'short catechism' is that there was also a longer catechism in use written by the same author, Alexander Nowell, so it was necessary to specify which catechism was meant.

In the rubrics at the end of the Prayer Book catechism, the responsibility for ensuring that those who come for confirmation are able to do these things is given to the parish minister (the 'curate' – that is the person who has the care or 'cure' of souls in a particular place). The curate offers the names of the suitable candidates to the bishop prior to the service.

The reason why this discipline regarding confirmation is said to be 'convenient' (in other words, 'appropriate) is that it is only once they know the basics of the faith as contained in the Creed, the basics of Christian behaviour as outlined in the Ten Commandments, and the basics of prayer as set forth in the Lord's Prayer, that those who are to be confirmed will be in a position to ratify the promises made for them at their baptism and promise to endeavour to keep them in future.

As Colquhoun notes, the word 'endeavour' has a slightly different meaning in the preface from what it commonly means today. As he says, in the preface it means:

> ...not to try hard (as nowadays) but to regard as a duty. What the preface is really saying at this point is that those who have been confirmed should regard it as their solemn duty to live their lives in accordance with their Christian profession.[5]

It is also important to note the reference in the preface to 'the Grace of God.' It is not said that the confirmation candidates shall promise to regard it as their duty to keep the baptismal vows in their own strength, but by 'the Grace of God,' which in this context means the strength which God will give them

---

[5] Colquhoun, *Catechism and Confirmation*, 174.

through the Holy Spirit in response to the prayers made during the confirmation service.

In the preface 'discretion' means 'discernment.' Those who have 'come to the years of discretion' are thus those who are old enough to discern the meaning of what they are taught in their confirmation preparation and to discern their obligation both to believe the Christian faith and to order their lives in accordance with it. As a result, they are in a position to meaningfully ratify the promises made at their baptism and to sincerely desire prayer for spiritual strength for the future.

The candidates' promise and vow

Then shall the Bishop say,

DO ye here, in the presence of God, and of this Congregation, renew the solemn promise and vow that was made in your name at your Baptism; ratifying and confirming the same in your own persons, and acknowledging yourselves bound to believe and to do all those things, which your Godfathers and Godmothers then undertook for you?

And every one shall audibly answer,

I do.

In this section of the service the confirmation the candidates affirm their own personal acceptance of the promises that were made for them at their baptism by their 'Godfathers and Godmothers'.

These promises are set out in the catechism, which reminds candidates for confirmation that their godparents made three promises on their behalf:

> First, that I should renounce the devil and all his works, the pomps and vanity of this wicked world, and all the sinful lusts of the flesh. Secondly, that I should believe all the articles of the Christian faith. And thirdly, that I should keep God's holy will and commandments, and walk in the same all the days of my life.

In the words of the preface, this part of the confirmation service gives the candidates the opportunity to 'ratify and confirm' these promises, the meaning of which has been explained to them in the catechism and also to 'promise, that by the grace of God they will evermore endeavour themselves faithfully to observe such things, as they by their own confession have assented unto.'

As John Stott puts it, the confirmation service says to the candidates:

> You can no longer rest under the umbrella of your God-parents. They cannot go on standing proxy for you. At your baptism they promised that you would renounce sin, trust in God and Jesus Christ, and obey his will in your life. That is to say, they promised that you would become a true Christian. The time has now come for you to make up your own mind. You can either repudiate what they promised in your name, or confirm it.

> You are old enough to decide thoughtfully and definitely that you want to follow Christ and belong to him. But it is not enough to make this decision privately and secretly on your own. The Church gives you the opportunity publicly and openly, in the presence of God and before your family, your friends and the whole local congregation, to nail your colours to the mast and declare yourself to be now on the Lord's side.[6]

The candidates affirm the promises made on their behalf with just two words 'I do' – but as Colquhoun notes:

> ...there is a whole world of meaning in those two monosyllables. They are like the 'I will' uttered by the bridegroom and bride in the marriage service which binds them together for life. In the same way the idea of confirmation binds the candidate to God forever.
>
> Think of what is involved in those two words. They are not only a momentary act of faith and dedication. They also represent a new attitude to the whole of life. They link up directly with the three vows of baptism, so that what the candidate is really saying is something like this:

---

[6] John Stott, *Your Confirmation* (London: Hodder & Stoughton, 1973), 9.

'Henceforth this will be my attitude to all this is false and evil, whether in myself or in the world outside: I will turn from it and renounce it.

Henceforth this shall be my attitude to God's truth revealed in his son Jesus Christ: I will embrace it and hold it fast.

Henceforth this should be my attitude to what I know to be God's way for me: I will follow it under his orders.'

All this is wrapped up in the purposeful avowal, *I do.*

Confirmation is commitment for life.[7]

While someone who is married can break their married vows, they are forever the person who made them. In the same way, it is possible for people who are confirmed subsequently to break their confirmation promise. However, they will always be the person who made this promise, and they need to be aware that God will hold them accountable on this basis at the day of judgement. They have said 'I do' and God will ask 'Did you?'

The versicles and responses

The Bishop. Our help is in the Name of the Lord;
Answer. Who hath made heaven and earth.
Bishop. Blessed be the Name of the Lord;
Answer. Henceforth world without end.

---

[7] Colquhoun, *Catechism and Confirmation*, 175–76.

> *Bishop.* Lord, hear our prayers;
> *Answer.* And let our cry come unto thee.

'I do' having been said, the service move on to the confirmation itself. This part of the service starts with a series of three versicles and responses said by the bishop and the congregation. They use words from three of the Psalms.

The first uses the words of Psalm 124:8.

> Our help is in the name of the LORD,
> who made heaven and earth.

The second uses the words of Psalm 113:2.

> Blessed be the name of the LORD
> From this time forth for evermore.

The third uses the words of Psalm 102:1:

> Hear my prayer, O LORD:
> let my cry come unto thee.

The function of these versicles and responses is to form a liturgical bridge between the making of the confirmation promise and the prayers that follow.

As we have noted, the preface to the service has already pointed out that those who are confirmed will need God's help ('the grace of God') to fulfil what they have promised. The first versicle and response reiterates this point by affirming that the help the candidates will need in the light of the promise they have just made comes from ('is in the name of') the God described in the Bible, the Lord who made heaven and earth.

Because God is the almighty creator who gives help to his people, his name is worthy of eternal praise, which is why the second versicle and response declares, 'Blessed be the name of the Lord; Henceforth world without end.'

Because this is who God is, we can also have confidence that he will hear our prayers. Hence the third versicle and response, 'Lord hear our prayers. And let our cry come unto thee.'

The confirmation prayers

> ALMIGHTY and ever-living God, who hast vouchsafed to regenerate these thy servants by Water and the Holy Ghost, and hast given unto them forgiveness of all their sins: Strengthen them, we beseech thee, O Lord, with the Holy Ghost the Comforter, and daily increase in them thy manifold gifts of grace; the spirit of wisdom and understanding; the spirit of counsel and ghostly strength; the spirit of knowledge and true godliness; and fill them, O Lord, with the spirit of thy holy fear, now and for ever. *Amen.*

> *Then all of them in order kneeling before the Bishop, he shall lay his hand upon the head of every one severally, saying,*

> DEFEND, O Lord, this thy Child [*or this thy Servant*] with thy heavenly grace, that he may continue thine for ever; and daily increase in thy Holy Spirit, more and more, until he come unto thy everlasting kingdom. *Amen.*

Following the versicles and responses the service moves on to the two confirmation prayers themselves.

The first prayer begins by describing God as 'almighty and ever-living'. This description is important because it set out the basis on which it is possible to have confidence that God can do what the bishop is going to ask him to do. If God were not almighty, he might not have the power to do it, and if he were not 'ever-living', there might come a time when he was no longer around to do it. However, neither of these things is true. God is always there, and he is always all-powerful, therefore we can have confidence that God can perform what the bishop is going to pray for.

The prayer then goes on to recall what God has already done for the candidates. At their baptism, though the work of the Holy Spirit, he has given them new life in union with Jesus and, on this basis, he has also forgiven them all their sins. The reason their sins are forgiven is that the union with Jesus means not only the start of a new life, but also the end of our old sinful life. This truth is emphasised by Paul in Romans 6:5–11 where he describes how baptism involves union with Jesus in both his death and resurrection and consequently being both dead to sin and alive to God:

> For if we have been united with him in a death like his, we shall certainly be united with him in a resurrection like his. We know that our old self was crucified with him so that the sinful body might be destroyed, and we might no longer be enslaved to sin. For he who has died is freed from sin. But if we have died with Christ, we believe that we shall also live with him. For we know that

> Christ being raised from the dead will never die again; death no longer has dominion over him. The death he died he died to sin, once for all, but the life he lives he lives to God. So you also must consider yourselves dead to sin and alive to God in Christ Jesus.

It is important at this point to note that the confirmation service follows the teaching of Scripture and the Fathers by talking about an *additional* gifting by the Spirit. As Michael Green writes, 'there is no scriptural justification for the notion that the person coming to confirmation receives the gift of the Holy Spirit then and there for the first time' and the confirmation service entertains no such idea.[8] On the contrary, the bishop declares that those who are going to be confirmed have already received the Spirit, which is why they have the new life of God already present within them.

To quote Colquhoun again:

> There is no suggestion here or in what follows that through the laying on of hands there is to be an initial gift of the Spirit, to those who have not a yet received him. Rather, as it has been said, the prayer admirably brings out what is the true idea of confirmation: "viz the 'strengthening' and the 'increase' of the spiritual life, already implanted, to full maturity.'[9]

---

[8] Michael Green, *Baptism* (London: Hodder and Stoughton, 1987), 103.
[9] Colquhoun, *Catechism and Confirmation*, 178.

In a tradition going back at least as far as Ambrose of Milan in the fourth century, the strengthening that is prayed for has a very specific shape.[10] What is prayed for is that those who are confirmed will received the sevenfold gifts of the Spirit prophesied in Isaiah 11:2–3.

If we ask why it is these gifts that are being asked for the answer is simple. Through the work of the Spirit those who have been baptised have 'put on Christ' (Gal 3:27). We have been united with Jesus. He is vine of which we are the branches (John 15:5). We are the body of which he is the head (Col 1:18). What follows from this fact is that just as Jesus was given the sevenfold gifts of the Spirit to enable him to fulfil his ministry as the Messiah, so also we need to be strengthened with those same sevenfold gifts if we are to continue his ministry in the world as those who are his body. In the great phrase of C S Lewis, we are 'little Christs' and we need the sevenfold gifts of the Spirit to fulfil that role.[11]

If we want to know about the nature of each of the gifts, a helpful explanation is given by Arthur Hall in his book on confirmation.[12] He describes the nature of the gifts as follows:

- The Spirit of Wisdom: ...In opposition to the folly of the world which says, in heart and life if not in word, 'There is no God' [Psalm 53:1], this Wisdom bids us 'lift up our hearts unto the Lord' and take Almighty God into account as the Alpha and Omega of all things, from

---

[10] Ambrose, 'On the Mysteries,' in *The Nicene and Post-Nicene Fathers*, Vol X (Edinburgh and Grand Rapids: T&T Clark/Eerdmans, 1997), 322.
[11] C. S. Lewis, *Mere Christianity* (Glasgow: Fount, 1984), 167.
[12] Arthur Hall, *Confirmation* (London: Longman, Green and Co., 1900), 152–162.

Whom we come, to Whom we go, the Source and End of our life, our Creator and our Judge. It teaches us to penetrate beneath the surface, and distinguish between things temporal and eternal, material and spiritual, visible and invisible.

- The Spirit of Understanding: ...The Spirit of Understanding raises our mind to the divine nature and its operations, penetrates into the meaning of Holy Scripture, shows us what is the bearing of the articles of the Creed on our conduct, how to build up our moral and spiritual life on the foundation of our holy faith [Jude 20].

- The Spirit of Counsel: ...The Spirit of Counsel directs us to make a right choice as to the use of means for attaining the end which wisdom sets before us, for carrying out the lessons which understanding teaches ... It corresponds with that 'discerning of spirits' of which we read in the New Testament [1 Cor 12:10] enabling us to distinguish between real and apparent good, guarding us against the craft and subtlety of the evil one, who disguises himself as an angel of light to deceive us with plausible but fallacious suggestions [2 Cor 11:14].

- The Spirit of Ghostly Strength: This is the complement to the Spirit of Counsel. The one guards us against the crafts of the subtle serpent, the other with the violent assaults of the roaring lion. The Spirit of Counsel enables us to perceive and know what things we ought to do; the Spirit of Ghostly Strength gives us grace and power faithfully to fulfil the same.

- The Spirit of Knowledge: This is distinct from Wisdom, from Understanding, and from Counsel. It is a higher gift, less intellectual, more spiritual. It describes a knowledge more personal, more intimate, more experimental. It may be thought of as corresponding rather with the intuitions of S. John than with the reasoned out conclusions of S. Paul, or to be represented by the declaration of S. Paul near the end of his life, 'I know whom I have believed' [2 Timothy 1:12].

- The Spirit of Godliness: ...This gift [also known as 'Piety']... we should understand as leading to the loving fulfilment of our duty towards God, and towards our neighbour for His sake as being children of a common Father... Addressing God as our Father, we are to live before him in an attitude of filial trust and love. Our obedience is not to be rendered in a grudging spirit as if He were a hard taskmaster, and we were bent on evading His commandments so far as we could or dared. Not 'Must I?' but rather 'May I?' or, if that sound weak, 'Ought I?' should be the question with which we approach duties.

- The Spirit of Holy Fear: ...This is indeed the seal clasping, as it were, the three preceding pairs of gifts, and ensuring perseverance as it guards against presumption. There is a fear of ourselves, rising from a knowledge of our frailty and a realisation of the perils to which we are exposed ... But it is not only, nor perhaps so much, the fear of ourselves that is included in the gift of Holy Fear, as the reverential fear of God. This is in no way incompatible with that filial spirit of love which we have considered under the title of

Godliness or Piety. Rather it is closely linked therewith; even as in the Lord's Prayer we are taught immediately after the address to our Father Who is in heaven to bow in worship before His majesty and say, 'Hallowed be Thy Name.' Loving intimacy is not shown in a rude or careless tossing about of sacred names, or in taking liberties with Almighty God. On the contrary, there will be a fear of losing Him Whom we have learned to prize, a fear of grieving Him Whom we have learned to love.

These seven gifts are the key to living a godly life. A careful study of the Gospels shows that these seven gifts were present in Jesus as a consequence of his anointing by the Spirit and that he perfectly exercised them. The prayer made by the bishop at confirmation is that through the work of the Holy Spirit these gifts will 'daily increase' in those who are being confirmed so that their lives will become more and more like the life of Jesus. As this happens they will be more and more able to handle rightly any other gifts God may choose to give them by his Spirit, using them to serve God and other people (rather than as a means of self-assertion) and using them wisely (in other words, in a way that is appropriate in a particular situation).

The second prayer, which constitutes the actual act of confirmation, is said by the bishop to each of the confirmation candidates individually as he lays his hand on their head. The word 'servant' is given as alternative to 'child' for use when there are adult candidates.

As Richard Hooker explains, the laying on of hands is way of symbolically focusing a prayer for God's blessing on the person being prayed for. In his words:

> With prayers of spiritual and personal benediction the manner hath been in all ages to use imposition of hands, as a ceremony betokening our restrained desires to the party, whom we present unto God in prayer.[13]

As is made clear later on in the service, the biblical precedent for the laying on hands by the bishop in confirmation is what takes place in Acts 8 and 19. The laying on of hands by Peter, John and Paul is an outward sign of their prayer that the Samaritans and the disciples at Ephesus will receive a further gifting by the Spirit after their baptism. In the confirmation service the bishop is doing exactly the same thing.

The bishop has previously asked God to strengthen the candidates through the Holy Spirit. Now he asks God to 'defend' them. The link between the two prayers is this: by being strengthened through their possession and exercise of the sevenfold gifts of the Spirit, those being confirmed will be defended against the assaults upon them from their own fallen natures, from the world around them, and from the activity of the devil.

In the words of Faustus of Riez, the bishop is asking is for God to strengthen the candidates 'by equipping them with fitting arms for the battle.'[14]

If we go back to the New Testament, we find that it is the power of the Spirit given to him after his baptism that Jesus battles

---

[13] Richard Hooker, *The Laws of Ecclesiastical Polity*, Bk.V. LXVI.1 in *The Works of Richard Hooker*, vol. 2 (Oxford: OUP, 1841), 71.
[14] Faustus of Riez in Wirgman, Doctrine of Confirmation, p.253.

successfully against Satan. Thus, Luke tells us that following his baptism and subsequent anointing with the Spirit:

> Jesus, full of the Holy Spirit, returned from the Jordan, and was led by the Spirit for forty days in the wilderness, tempted by the devil (Luke 4:1–2).

The point made here by Luke, in contrast to the accounts of Jesus' temptation in Matthew 4:1 and Mark 1:12, is that Jesus was not only led into the wilderness to do battle with Satan, but that he was also led by the Spirit in the course of that battle.

In the words of Swete: 'it cannot be doubted that the Spirit which urged the Lord to the conflict with Satan strengthened Him for it and carried Him through.'[15] As Swete goes on to say, the presence of the Spirit is shown:

> in the insight which discerns the subtle danger that underlies an apparently innocent exercise of Messianic power: in the strength of will which resists the impatience that grasps at an end without regard to the means by which the end is reached; in the humility which, though fully conscious of a unique relation to God, refuses while in the flesh to transcend the limits of mortal weakness. In all this we may reverently recognize the hand of the Spirit of God upholding and guiding the humanity of our Lord, and giving promise to us of like

---

[15] Henry Swete, *The Holy Spirit in the New Testament* (London: Macmillan, 1910), 54.

> support and direction in our own temptations.[16]

If we turn from the Gospels to Acts, we find that it is the power of the same Spirit, poured out on the apostles at Pentecost, that enables the members of the Early Church to triumph in the same way in the battles they have to face. For example, in Acts 4, the apostles Peter and John are told by the Jewish authorities to stop preaching about Jesus. However, they and the church as whole, are given 'boldness' through the Spirit to continue with their preaching in spite of this opposition (Acts 4:8, 13, 31).

What the examples in Luke 4 and Acts 4 show is that God's defence of his people is an active defence. He does not prevent temptation or opposition coming their way, but he does give them the necessary power (the 'fitting arms for the battle') through the Spirit to triumph against the challenges they are facing. It this active defence by God of his people which is being asked for when the bishop prays 'Defend, O Lord.'

As Colquhoun notes, it is also important to note the repetition in this prayer of the words 'daily increase' already used in the previous prayer. As he writes, this repetition:

> serves to emphasize that the Christian life – the new life in the Spirit – is meant to be a progressive experience. In fact, the Christian life is always a pilgrim's progress, and this prayer used at the imposition of hands might almost be described as a pilgrim's prayer. It asks that the Christian who has boldly made confession of his faith may be guarded by God's grace as he goes

---

[16] Swete, *Holy Spirit in New Testament,* 54–55.

forward on the journey; that he may press on with unfaltering step along the road, and that he may accordingly be strengthened by the Holy Spirit in ever increasing measure until he reaches his journey's end. This is a prayer for protection, perseverance and progress in the Christian life.[17]

Although he was not referring to this confirmation prayer, John Bunyan accurately describes its meaning his account of Christian's visit to the Interpreter's house in *The Pilgrim's Progress*.

In this account, Bunyan says:

> Then I saw in my dream that the Interpreter took Christian by the hand, and led him into a place where was fire burning against a wall, and one standing by it, always casting much water upon it, to quench; yet did the fire burn higher and hotter.[18]

Christian asks what this sight meant and the Interpreter answers:

> This fire is the work of grace that is wrought in the heart; he that casts water upon it to extinguish it and put it out, is the devil: but in that thou seest the fire not withstanding burn higher and hotter, thou shalt also see the reason of that. So he had him about the

---

[17] Colquhoun, *Catechism and Confirmation*, 179.
[18] John Bunyan, *The Pilgrim's Progress* (London: Religious Tract Society, N.D.), 40.

backside of the wall, where he saw a man with a vessel of oil in his hand which he did also continually cast (but secretly) into the fire.[19]

Christian again asks the meaning of what he has just seen and the Interpreter replies:

> This is Christ, who continually, with the oil of His grace, maintains the work already begun in the heart; by the means of which, notwithstanding all the devil can do, the souls of his people prove gracious still. And in that that thou sawest that the man stood behind the wall to maintain the fire; this is to teach thee, that it is hard for the tempted to see how this work of grace is maintained in the soul.[20]

When in the confirmation service the bishop prays 'Defend, O Lord' this is a prayer that the oil of grace given through Christ, that is to say the Holy Spirit, will be poured continually into the souls of those who are being confirmed so that, in spite of the devil's attempts to prevent it, their faith and love for God will continually burn 'higher and hotter' throughout their earthly pilgrimage until they finally come safely to their journey's end. It is in this way that, as the prayer says, 'they will continue thine for ever.'

---

[19] Bunyan, *Pilgrim's Progress,* 40–41.
[20] Bunyan, *Pilgrim's Progress,* 41.

The mutual salutation

Then shall the Bishop say,

Bishop. The Lord be with you.
Answer. And with thy spirit.

And (all kneeling down) the Bishop shall add,
Let us pray.

The final section of the service, consisting of further prayers led by the bishop for those who have just been confirmed, and for the congregation as a whole, begins with what is known as the mutual salutation.

In this part of the service, the bishop and the congregation greet each other with a traditional greeting which expresses what Christians should most desire for one another, namely that 'The Lord be with you.' The words 'with you' do not refer to geographical location. What is expressed is the hope that God will present *for* you, giving you everything you need to sustain you on your pilgrimage through this world to the world to come. 'With you' and 'with thy spirit' are two ways of saying the same thing since 'spirit' with a small 's' is another word for someone's 'soul' or 'self'.

The Lord's Prayer

OUR Father which art in heaven, Hallowed be thy Name, Thy kingdom come, Thy will be done, in earth as it is in heaven. Give us this day our daily bread; And forgive us our trespasses, As we forgive them that trespass

against us; And lead us not into temptation,
But deliver us from evil. Amen.

As in the services of Baptism and Holy Communion in the *Book of Common Prayer,* the Lord's Prayer in the confirmation service forms an introduction to the final prayers at the end of the service. It is used for this purpose because it is the prayer given to the church by Jesus himself and comprehensively sums up all that Christians need to pray for (which is why it is the prayer taught in the catechism). The reason the Doxology at the end of the Lord's Prayer is omitted here is because the prayer precedes further petitions rather than preceding thanksgiving.

The first collect

And this Collect.

ALMIGHTY and ever-living God, who makest us both to will and to do those things that be good and acceptable unto thy divine Majesty; We make our humble supplications unto thee for these thy servants, upon whom (after the example of thy holy Apostles) we have now laid our hands, to certify them (by this sign) of thy favour and gracious goodness towards them. Let thy fatherly hand, we beseech thee, ever be over them; let thy Holy Spirit ever be with them; and so lead them in the knowledge and obedience of thy Word, that in the end they may obtain everlasting life; through our Lord Jesus Christ, who with

thee and the Holy Ghost liveth and reigneth,
ever one God, world without end. *Amen.*

This collect begins by acknowledging the nature of God and his activity. God is almighty – that is, the one who has the power to always achieve his good purposes. He is also 'everlasting' – the God who is always there to exercise this power.

What God does is cause us 'to will and to do' the things that are pleasing in his sight. Our good works are *our* good works, because they are the works that we will to do, and then perform. However, we *will* them and *do* them because God causes us to do so. The biblical basis for this section of the collect is the words of Paul in Philippians 2:12–13:

> Therefore, my beloved, as you have always obeyed, so now, not only as in my presence but much more in my absence, work out your own salvation with fear and trembling; for God is at work in you, both to will and to work for his good pleasure.

The collect then moves on to a petition for those who have just been confirmed, describing them as those: 'upon whom (after the example of thy holy Apostles) we have now laid our hands, to certify them (by this sign) of thy favour and gracious goodness towards them.'

The reference to 'the example of thy holy Apostles' is a reference to Acts 8:14–17 and 19:6 in which Peter and John lay their hands on the converts in Samaria and Paul lays his hands on the disciples in Ephesus. In line with the belief of the church in the Patristic and Medieval periods, the Church of England has traditionally believed that the action of the bishop in laying on hands in confirmation is in direct continuity with the action of the apostles in these two chapters. The apostles established the practice of laying of hands on those who had been baptised as a form of prayer for the further gifting of the Spirit, and the Early Church continued this practice with the bishop exercising this specific aspect of the apostolic role.[21] At the Reformation, the reformed Church of England simply maintained what had always been done, stripping out later accretions such as the anointing with chrism.

In the words of the seventeenth-century writer Jeremy Taylor:

> The bishops were always and the only ministers of Confirmation. This was the constant practice and doctrine of the Primitive Church, and derived from the practice and tradition of the apostles, and recorded in the Acts written by S. Luke. For this is our great rule in this case, what they did in rituals and consigned to posterity is our example and warranty; we see it done thus, and by these men, and by no others, and no otherwise, and we have no authority, and no reason to go another way.[22]

---

[21] It is important to note that the Early Church did not confuse bishops and apostles. What it held was that certain specific aspects of the apostolic role (such as the overall pastoral responsibility for the local churches and ordination) which had been delegated during the apostles' lifetimes to leaders such as James, Timothy and Titus, were exercised in turn by the early bishops after the apostles had died, the first bishops having been appointed by the apostles themselves. The laying on hands by the bishops was simply another aspect of this pattern.

[22] Jeremy Taylor, *Discourse of Confirmation*, section IV, in Hall, *Confirmation*, 45–46.

The words 'to certify them (by this sign) of thy favour and gracious goodness towards them' were objected to by the Puritans at the Savoy Conference in 1661 on the grounds that 'this seems to speak it a sacrament' whereas (as we have seen) Article XVV declares that confirmation is not a sacrament.[23]

What this objection fails to understand is what sort of a sign confirmation is. In baptism and Holy Communion the use of material elements (water and bread and wine) is an outward sign of divine grace and so is the laying on hands at confirmation. However, the difference is that in baptism and Holy Communion what is signified is the divine grace given through the material elements to be received by faith, whereas in the case of confirmation what the laying on of hands certifies is the willingness of God to answer prayer, and specifically to answer prayer for the gift of the Holy Spirit. In the words of Luke 11:13 'If you then, who are evil, know how to give good gifts to your children, how much more will the heavenly Father give the Holy Spirit to those who ask him!' To put it another way, what the laying on of episcopal hands says to the confirmation candidates is that you can be sure that God will answer prayer for the strengthening gift of the Holy Spirit because (a) God has said he will answer prayer for the Holy Spirit and (b) we have biblical examples of his answer to such prayer in Acts 8 and 19.

The second half of the collect goes on to ask three things for the newly confirmed:

- That they will receive God's fatherly care and protection for the rest of their lives

---

[23] Edward Cardwell, *A History of Conferences and other proceedings* (Oxford: OUP, 1849), 329.

- That the Holy Spirit will abide with them forever in accordance with Jesus' promise in John 14:16
- That under the Spirit's guidance they will grow in their knowledge of and obedience to what God says in the Bible so that instructed by God through its teaching they may eventually attain eternal life

Overall, as Colquhoun observes, the collect:

> looks to the future and makes clear that the significance of confirmation is not limited to the time of its administration. What happens at that one moment is intended to represent every succeeding moment. Henceforth (so the prayer seems to say to those confirmed) all your life should be like this: kept by God's power, filled with his Spirit, guided safely along the road that leads to everlasting life.[24]

It is for this comprehensive divine blessing that the bishop prays in this collect, that the confirmed claim as their own when they say 'Amen,' and that the confirmed should go on claiming throughout the rest of their lives.

The second collect

> O ALMIGHTY Lord, and everlasting God, vouchsafe, we beseech thee, to direct, sanctify, and govern both our hearts and bodies, in the ways of thy laws, and in the works of thy commandments; that through

---

[24] Colquhoun, *Catechism and Confirmation*, 181.

thy most mighty protection, both here and ever, we may be preserved in body and soul; through our Lord and Saviour Jesus Christ. *Amen.*

This second collect, which is a prayer for all present at the service, is another prayer for comprehensive blessing.

As in the previous collect, and for the same reason, God is referred to as 'Almighty and everlasting' and what he is asked to do is to 'direct, sanctify, and govern both our hearts and bodies, in the ways of thy laws, and in the works of thy commandments.' 'Our hearts and bodies' means us in the entirety of who we are, and what the collect is asking is that through his Spirit, God should 'direct' us (in other words, show us how we should live), 'sanctify' us (make us people willing to live in this way) and 'govern' us (so arrange the circumstances of our lives by his providential care that we can live the life God wants us to live).

The collect specifies that how we should live is in 'the ways of thy laws, and in the works of thy commandments.' The 'ways of thy laws' means the general principles for human behaviour laid down the Bible and 'the works of thy laws' means the specific actions which are demanded by these principles. What this means, in other words, is that to live rightly before him we need God to give us an overall understanding of what he requires from us and specific insight as to what we need to do at any given moment in time. What the collect is asking is that through his Spirit, God will grant us this understanding and insight.

As in the previous prayers in the service, the background to this collect is the reality of spiritual warfare. The world, the flesh and the devil will combine to try to prevent us from living in obedience to God's ways and laws (see Genesis 3 and the stories of Jesus' temptations in the wilderness). Consequently, the collect (like the bishop's second confirmation prayer) asks for God's protection so that we may be preserved from harm in 'body and soul' (that is, in the entirety of our being).

The reason why in both this collect and in the previous prayer is offered 'though Jesus Christ' is because, as Hebrews teaches us, he is the great High Priest who represents us before God the Father and the reason our prayers are heard is because of what he has done us and who we are in him.

> For we have not a high priest who is unable to sympathize with our weaknesses, but one who in every respect has been tempted as we are, yet without sin. Let us then with confidence draw near to the throne of grace, that we may receive mercy and find grace to help in time of need (Heb 4:15–16).

It is through Jesus that we are able to come in prayer to God as our Father with the confidence that he will hear and answer out prayers.

The final blessing

Then the Bishop shall bless them, saying thus,

THE blessing of God Almighty, the Father, the Son, and the Holy Ghost, be upon you, and remain with you, for ever. *Amen.*

The service concludes with the blessing of the congregation by the bishop. The blessing which is invoked in these words is a blessing from the Triune God, Father, Son and Holy Spirit. In context, the specific blessing which is in mind is that this God will grant to those present, both now and in the future, the things that have been asked for in the service and have been signified by the laying on of hands.

The rubric concerning admission to Communion

> *And there shall none be admitted to the holy Communion, until such time as he be confirmed, or be ready and desirous to be confirmed.*

As the *Tutorial Prayer Book* notes, it is important to understand what is (and is not) said in this rubric.[25]

1. The rubric does not contemplate admission to Holy Communion of unconfirmed members of the Church of England, save when confirmation is desired and purposed and opportunity only is wanting.[26]

---

[25] Charles Neil and J. M. Willoughby, *The Tutorial Prayer Book* (London: The Harrison Trust, 1913).

[26] At the time this rubric was put into its present form in 1662 there were a large number of people who had never had the opportunity to be confirmed because of the absence of bishops during the Civil War and the Commonwealth, and this form of the rubric was designed to allow them the opportunity to receive Communion without having to wait to be confirmed.

2. The rubric, nevertheless, teaches by plain implication that the rite, as such, is not essential to fitness for partaking of Holy Communion.

3. The rubric, even its even in its unqualified form of 1552, certainly did not contemplate the exclusion of members of churches not subject to the ecclesiastical ordinances of the Church of England.[27]

To put it simply, the rubric is a Church of England ordinance concerning the normal rules for admission to Communion in the Church of England. It is not concerned with the status of members of other churches.

In the rubric, for someone to be ready to be confirmed means that they have been instructed in, and give their consent to, the teaching contained in the Prayer Book catechism.

---

[27] Neil and Willoughby, *Tutorial Prayer Book*, 437.

Chapter 4:

Questions about confirmation today

In the final chapter of this study we shall look at the answers to a number of questions that are often asked about confirmation today.

What is the difference between baptism and confirmation?

As we have seen in the course of this study, the difference between baptism and confirmation is that action of the Spirit in baptism grants us new life in Christ and the forgiveness of our sins. At confirmation, we are given the gifts of the Spirit, and particularly the sevenfold gifts prophesied in Isaiah 11:2–3, to strengthen us as we live for God and engage in battle against the world, the flesh and the devil.

The way in which confirmation thus differs from baptism is well summarised by Hooker who explains that the Fathers of the Church attribute to confirmation:

> that gift or grace of the Holy Ghost, not which first maketh us Christian men, but when we are made such assisteth us in all virtue, armeth us against temptation and sin.[1]

---

[1] Hooker, *Laws of Ecclesiastical Polity*, Bk. V. lxvi.5 in *Works*, Vol. II, 73.

Should I get confirmed if I have been baptised as an adult?

If you have been baptised as an adult, confirmation is obviously not necessary as an occasion for you to ratify the promises made on your behalf when you were baptised as an infant. However, it is important for you to be confirmed in order that you can ask for and receive the strengthening gift of the Holy Spirit which God wants to give you now you have been baptised.

Is it right to think of confirmation in terms of 'baptism in the Holy Spirit?'

Some Christians in the Pentecostal and Charismatic traditions, in common with Anglo-Catholic theologians such as Mason and Dix, have argued that 'Baptism in the Holy Spirit' refers to a gift of the Holy Spirit which is given separately from baptism.[2] In their view, a person is baptised with water and then subsequently receives baptism in the Holy Spirit.

However, the New Testament evidence does not support this argument. As Green correctly notes there are only seven references to baptism in the Spirit in the New Testament – 'no more and no less'.[3] These references are Matthew 3:11, Mark 1:8, Luke 3:16, John 1:33, Acts 1:5, Acts 11:15–16 and 1 Corinthians 12:13. In all these references, 'baptism' means water baptism and 'baptism in the Spirit' means the gift of the Spirit given at the same time as water baptism. In addition, water baptism and the gift of the Spirit are also linked in John

---

[2] See for example the definition of Baptism in the Spirit by the American Assemblies of God at
ag.org/Beliefs/Position-Papers/Baptism-in-the-Holy-Spirit
[3] Green, *Baptism*, 133.

3:5, Acts 2:38, 1 Corinthians 6:11, Galatians 3:27–4:6, Ephesians 1:13–14 and Titus 3:5.

To make the same point another way, there is no verse in in the New Testament which uses the term 'baptism in the Spirit' to describe a gift of the Spirit that is not linked to baptism in water and no text that implies that there can be a Christian baptism that does not involve the gift of the Spirit.

All this means that it is a mistake to think of confirmation in terms of 'baptism in the Holy Spirit.' Baptism in the Holy Spirit has already taken place.

The key thing in confirmation is that the baptismal promises are ratified and that hands are laid on with prayer for people to be strengthened with the sevenfold gift of the Spirit. Whether miraculous signs take place is a secondary matter. We should praise God if they do take place, but not be concerned if they do not.

Should we expect to have a spiritual experience at confirmation?

Some people do have a profound spiritual experience when they are confirmed. For example, Green records the following testimony from the Anglican nun, Sister Margaret Magdalen:

> For a long time I had prayed for baptism in the Spirit, and felt puzzled and grieved that God did not appear to respond to this prayer. Then, when I became an Anglican, I was confirmed. The only sense I could make of confirmation at that stage in my life, when I had been a committed Christian and indeed a missionary for many years, was to see it as part of, and all of a piece with, my

> baptism (which had been as a believer by immersion).
>
> So I prepared for confirmation as a deepening of the initial baptism, laying hold of that grace within the sacrament with firm hands. As the confirmation service proceeded, I became full of a radiant joy which simply overflowed – I couldn't contain it. I didn't sleep a wink that night because I was filled with praise and joy sometimes poured forth in tongues and sometimes took me in to a deep contemplative silence.
>
> Next day my students were awed when I began to teach them. When I asked them why they were so subdued, they told me they were afraid of the shining of my face. Like Moses I did not know I shone. [4]

The point to note, however, is that such experiences are comparatively rare. Most people who are confirmed do not report having this sort of experience. Nevertheless, this does not mean that there was something missing from their confirmation. It simply means that God decided that in their case this experience was not necessary.

The fundamental points to grasp in relation to confirmation and our experience are that:

1. The basis for our assurance that God will give us the sevenfold gifts of the Spirit is not any experience we

---

[4] Green, *Baptism*, 140–141.

may or may not have had, but the words of Jesus 'how much more will the heavenly Father give the Holy Spirit to those who ask' (Luke 11:13). At confirmation we and others ask, so we can be confident that God will give.

2. We can know that we have received the Spirit at confirmation because we find that we 'daily increase' in the sevenfold gifts – in wisdom, understanding, counsel, Ghostly strength, knowledge, Godliness and holy fear. It is this daily increase that we should desire and if we do not (yet) see it happening in our lives then we should continue to pray that it will happen, trusting that we have a faithful God who gives his people what he has promised.

Which confirmation service should we use?

The 1662 confirmation service remains authorised for use and constitutes the key theological benchmark for the Church of England's understanding of confirmation. For the Church of England, it is still the case that confirmation is what the 1662 service says it is.

However, the 1662 service is not the one that is generally used in the Church of England today. The confirmation rite that is generally used is the one that is found in the initiation services in *Common Worship*.

This rite contains the key elements of a confirmation rite:

- It gives candidates the opportunity to affirm their faith, their repentance, their rejection of the devil and all rebellion against God and their commitment to follow Jesus.

- It acknowledges that the help we need comes from God.
- It acknowledges that the candidates have received new birth and the forgiveness of sins at baptism.
- It contains the laying on hands by the bishop with prayers for the candidates to receive the sevenfold gifts of the Spirit and to 'daily increase' in them.

Nevertheless, the *Common Worship* rite is less satisfactory than the 1662 service for a number of reasons:

- There is no explicit recognition that those who have been baptised as infants are ratifying the promises made on their behalf by their godparents.
- In the versicles and responses, the key words 'Lord hear our prayers ... And let our cry come unto thee' are omitted.
- There is no reference to the 'gifts of grace' in the opening prayer in the *Common Worship* rite.
- The words used in *Common Worship*, 'Let your Holy Spirit rest upon them', are less theologically precise than the equivalent words in the 1662 service: 'Strengthen them, we beseech thee, O Lord with the Holy Ghost the Comforter.'
- There is no equivalent to the final collect in the 1662 service and the first collect only exists in an edited form as an optional prayer to be used in intercessions.

Because this is the case, it is better to use the 1662 service, if possible, on the grounds that one should want to use the best service available. However, since in most dioceses the

Common Worship rite is the one that is in general use, there may be no realistic possibility of using the 1662 service instead.

If this is the case, the best way forward may be for candidates to be taught the 1662 service as the basis for their theological understanding of confirmation, but for them to be then taught the *Common Worship* rite as well, with an explanation being given as to why it is permissible to make use of this form of confirmation service even though it is less satisfactory than the traditional confirmation liturgy.

If the language of the 1662 service is an initial stumbling block for candidates, it may be helpful for those instructing them to point them to the confirmation service in *An English Prayer Book* which is contained in Appendix A at the back of this study. This has the 1662 order of service, but in slightly updated language.

How should candidates best be prepared for confirmation?

Canon B27 sections 2 and 3 lays down that:

> Every minister who has a cure of souls shall diligently seek out children and other persons whom he shall think meet to be confirmed and shall use his best endeavour to instruct them in the Christian faith and life as set forth in the Holy Scriptures, *The Book of Common Prayer*, and the Church Catechism.
>
> The minister shall present none to the bishop but such as are come to years of discretion and can say the Creed, the Lord's

Prayer, and the Ten Commandments, and can also render an account of their faith according to the said Catechism.[5]

The best way to respond to this canonical requirement is to simply teach people the contents of the Prayer Book catechism (which is the catechism referred to in the Canon).

There are now other forms of Anglican catechetical material available.[6] However, it is arguable that these are not as useful as the Prayer Book catechism when it comes to providing a basic introduction to the Christian faith. This is either because they are not as theologically reliable as this catechism, or because they lack its brevity and clarity, or both.

It follows from this that there is a strong case for using to the catechism as a basis for teaching the fundamentals of the Christian faith in confirmation classes. It is short enough to be learned by heart and this remains an invaluable way of imprinting basic Christian truth in the candidates' hearts and minds.

It is true that some of the language in the catechism is now dated, such as the use of the word 'ghostly' when we would say 'spiritual' and the use of the word 'generally' when we would say 'universally'. However, there are not that many dated words used in the catechism and those that do exist can easily be explained when the meaning of the catechism is expounded. As before, *An English Prayer Book* is a useful resource because it has a version of the catechism in slightly updated English.

---

[5] *The Canons of the Church of England*, 7th edition, at https://www.churchofengland.org/more/policy-and-thinking/canons-church-england/section-b.

[6] See Appendix B in Davie, *Instruction in the Way of the Lord*.

It is also true that the baptismal promises referred to in the Catechism no longer correspond to the promises that are normally made at Baptism since the promises made in the *Common Worship* baptism services are different from those in the *Book of Common Prayer*. However, this too is not an insuperable difficulty. The point that needs to be made is that the promises referred to in the Catechism are promises which flow from the nature of baptism itself. It follows that everyone who has been baptised should be seeking to live out these promises, regardless of the specific words that were used when they were baptised.[7]

Having been instructed in the catechism, candidates should then be instructed in the confirmation service itself, using the 1662 service as the basis for the reasons explained previously, but with reference to the *Common Worship* rite as well as required.

What is the relationship between confirmation and admission to Holy Communion?

The general requirement of the Church of England, which, as we have seen, can be traced back through the Middle Ages to the Patristic period is that confirmation should precede admission to Holy Communion.

However, the Church of England also now allows a range of exceptions to this rule which go beyond the sole exception laid down in the rubric at the end of the 1662 confirmation service.

---

[7] Useful introductions to the *Prayer Book Catechism* can be found in Colquhoun, *Catechism and Confirmation*; Martin Davie, *Instruction In the Way of the Lord* (London: Latimer Trust, 2014); and Arthur Robinson, *The Church Catechism Explained* (Cambridge: CUP, 1903).

The current Church of England regulations on the matter can be found Canon B15A 'Of the admission to Holy Communion'. This Canon lays down:

> 1. There shall be admitted to the Holy Communion:
>
> (a) members of the Church of England who have been confirmed in accordance with the rites of that Church or are ready and desirous to be so confirmed or who have been otherwise episcopally confirmed with unction, or with the laying on of hands except as provided by the next following Canon;
>
> (b) baptized persons who are communicant members of other Churches which subscribe to the doctrine of the Holy Trinity, and who are in good standing in their own Church;
>
> (c) any other baptized persons authorized to be admitted under regulations of the General Synod; and
>
> (d) any baptized person in immediate danger of death.
>
> 2. If any person by virtue of sub-paragraph (b) above regularly receives the Holy Communion over a long period which appears likely to continue indefinitely, the minister shall set before him the normal

requirements of the Church of England for communicant status in that Church.

3. Where any minister is in doubt as to the application of this Canon, he shall refer the matter to the bishop of the diocese or other Ordinary and follow his guidance thereon.[8]

In these regulations, 'episcopally confirmed with unction' in 1(a) covers not only confirmation in the Roman Catholic Church, but also the chrismation of infants in Orthodox churches. Since 2006, 1(c) covers unconfirmed children who can now be admitted to Communion under the provisions of the 'Admission of Baptised Children to Holy Communion Regulations 2006' (these regulations can be found in Appendix B at the end of this study).

Is it right to admit unconfirmed children to Holy Communion?

The standard arguments for admitting unconfirmed children to Holy Communion are helpfully summarised in the section on 'Admission of Children to Holy Communion before Confirmation in the Diocese of Durham' on the Durham diocese website.[9]

The summary is as follows:

- Baptism is the undisputed rite of entry into membership of the Body of Christ: 'In the one Spirit

---

[8] *Canons of the Church of England*, 7th ed.
[9] Diocese of Durham, 'Admission of Children to Communion before Confirmation in the Diocese of Durham,' 2013, available at https://drive.google.com/file/d/1QURSVzhafnkOT21GGmosZIN2x2xjPpSt/view.

we were all baptised into one body' (*Common Worship*, p. 290); and membership of that body is affirmed in the reception of Holy Communion: 'we are one body, because we all share in one bread' (*Common Worship*, p. 179). To deny Holy Communion to any baptised Christian could be seen as denying the full validity of their Baptism.

- If a sacrament is seen as a free, unearned gift of grace expressing God's unconditional love, to what extent can conditions be imposed regarding admission to the sacrament of Holy Communion?

- Jesus uses children as an example of what 'the greatest in the kingdom of heaven' are like. How is this reflected in our practice if we make children the least at the Communion Table by denying their full participation? Some passages of Scripture to consider: Matthew 18:1–5; 19:13–14; 21:14–17.

- If confirmation is made a condition of receiving Holy Communion, it could be seen as having a confused significance – vying with baptism for importance as a rite of entry – rather than having a clear and distinct significance of its own as a rite of adult commitment.[10]

All these four points are problematic.

- It is true that baptism is the rite of entry into the body of Christ, but this of itself does not settle the issue of whether a baptised child should be admitted to Communion. The issue which needs to be decided is whether the fact of being a member of the body of

---

[10] Diocese of Durham, 'Admission of Children to Communion before Confirmation'.

Christ means automatically qualifies someone for admission to Holy Communion.

- It is true that a sacrament is an expression of God's unconditional love, but an appropriate response is required to that love as expressed in Holy Communion, and the question is whether a child is yet capable of making that response.

- It is true that Jesus made children an example of being 'the greatest in the kingdom of heaven,' but what has to be shown is how this relates to admission to Communion. After all, we do not allow a child to serve on a PCC, or be ordained, because children are 'the greatest in the kingdom of heaven.'

- Finally, it can be argued that it is precisely because of the significance of confirmation as a rite of adult commitment that it is the appropriate gateway to Holy Communion.

What the argument about the admission of children to Holy Communion really boils down to is the question of what the proper requirements are for someone to be admitted to Holy Communion and whether children can satisfy these requirements.

This point is well made by Roger Beckwith in his article 'The Age of Admission to Communion.'[11] Like the writer of the Durham material, he agrees that a key issue is the relation between baptism and admission to Communion, but he draws a different conclusion from this fact on the grounds that baptism is not complete without faith. Baptism is complete in

---

[11] Roger Beckwith, 'The Age of Admission to Communion,' *Churchman* 85 (1971).

terms of what God does, but it still requires a response from us.

Beckwith writes:

> Baptism, as we saw earlier, is indeed a prerequisite for admission to communion; and baptism, as we further observed, is not complete without faith. Faith, moreover, involves repentance (Mk. 1:15; Acts 20: 21; Heb. 6:1), and repentance is a mature decision about changing the course of one's life – a decision of which children may in some cases be capable, but of which we should not expect them to be capable and may not be able to distinguish whether they are or not. A communicant is, in sacramental terms, a committed and practising Christian: he has been baptised, which means that he has also been instructed in the word, has repented and has confessed his faith; and he is now living a life of obedience to God. But a child has hardly reached this stage. He may not yet be capable of a radical repentance, and the faith that he has is essentially immature and unstable: 'children', as St. Paul says, are 'tossed to and fro and carried about with every wind of doctrine' (Eph. 4:14). And though, in the context of a Christian family especially, there is every reason to hope that a child's incipient faith will survive the testing experience of growing up and that he

will make a mature decision against sin and for Christ, yet there does not seem to be any adequate reason for anticipating the outcome and treating him in a way which is beyond his years. The age of maturity is not an age that can be fixed with rigidity, and the Bible does not attempt to fix it in this way; but one need not hesitate to say that it is an age which a young child has certainly not reached, and which an adolescent may well not have reached either.[12]

The rationale for the traditional Church of England practice of making confirmation the gateway to Communion is precisely because, as we have already noted, confirmation involves making an act of adult commitment to Jesus Christ. This does not mean that confirmation should not take place until someone is 18, but what it does mean is that they should have reached what the Prayer Book calls the 'years of discretion' – that age when someone is capable of exercising 'their own responsible, independent judgement' (an age which will vary from person to person).[13] When they have reached this age, they are capable of being confirmed and, for the same reason, they are capable of the informed repentance, faith and charity which the Prayer Book lays down as the requirement for coming to Communion.[14]

---

[12] Beckwith, 'Age of Admission to Communion', 29–30. See also Roger Beckwith and Andrew Daunton-Fear, *The Water and the Wine: A Contribution to the Debate on Children and Holy Communion* (London: Latimer Trust, 2015).
[13] Colquhoun, *Catechism and Order of Confirmation*, 173.
[14] Question. What is required of those who come to the Lord's Supper? Answer. To examine themselves, whether they repent them

To put it another way, the age at which someone is capable of being confirmed is the same age when they are capable of meeting the requirements for admission to Communion – and the spiritual requirements in terms of repentance and faith are the same in both cases. Therefore, it makes perfect sense to say that people should not be admitted to Communion unless they are 'ready and desirous' for confirmation and, in normal circumstances, not until confirmation has taken place. If someone isn't ready for confirmation, then they are not ready for Holy Communion either.

How does the Church of England view confirmation in other churches?

The Church of England currently has an ambivalent attitude to confirmation in other churches.

On the one hand:

- It recognises with any equivocation Roman Catholic confirmation, and Orthodox chrismation.

- Under the terms of the House of Bishops' *Code of Practice on Co-operation by the Church of England with Other Churches,* the Church of England permits joint confirmation services with churches that practice presbyteral confirmation.[15]

On the other hand:

---

truly of their former sins, steadfastly purposing to lead a new life; have a lively faith in God's mercy though Christ, with a thankful remembrance of his death; and be in charity with all men. (*Prayer Book* catechism).
[15] The House of Bishops, *Code of Practice on Co-operation by the Church of England with Other Churches* (London: The Church of England, GS 2117, 2019).

- Under Canon B15A(2), the Church of England requires communicant members of other churches to consider being confirmed in the Church of England, even if they have already been confirmed in their own church., if they intend to receive communion in the Church of England 'over a long period which appears likely to continue indefinitely.'

- Under Canon B28(2), someone who has not been 'episcopally confirmed' but who wishes to be received into the Church of England has to undergo episcopal confirmation, even if they have already received presbyteral confirmation in another church. The same discipline applies for those from other churches who want to be ordained or become readers.[16]

What this means is that the Church of England is prepared to recognise the validity of presbyteral confirmation to the extent that it permits joint confirmation services in which presbyters take part alongside bishops, but, on the other hand, it does not recognise it when it comes to people taking Communion regularly in the Church of England, being received into the Church of England, or being qualified to be ordained, or to be Readers.

What would be more theologically coherent would be for the Church of England to recognise that there is a common pattern of confirmation which can be found in a range of different churches including the Roman Catholic Church and churches in the Old Catholic, Lutheran, Reformed, Moravian and Methodist traditions.

The elements in this pattern are:

---

[16] *Canons of the Church of England*, 7th ed.

- An affirmation of baptismal promises
- A Trinitarian profession of faith (mostly using the words of the Apostles' Creed)
- A prayer for God to strengthen the candidates through His Spirit often linked to the sevenfold gifting promised in Isaiah 11
- Some form of commitment to living the Christian life as part of the church
- The presiding minister laying his/her hand on the head of each candidate
- Some form of welcome to the newly confirmed by the members of the local Christian community

Furthermore, even though different forms of words are used, there is a striking similarity in the content of the reaffirmation of the baptismal promises, the profession of faith, the prayer for the gift of the Spirit, and the words accompanying the laying of the hand on the candidate's head.

What we are dealing with, in fact, is a series of variations on a common confirmation rite, a rite that has its roots behind the divisions of the Reformation and post-Reformation periods in the traditions of the undivided Western Church of the Patristic and Medieval periods.

Having recognised this common pattern, the Church of England should then go on to accept that confirmations that are performed according to this common pattern in fact possess all the necessary elements for a valid confirmation and therefore should not be repeated (any more than baptisms should be repeated).

The objection to this approach would of course be that it would involve recognising the validity of confirmations performed by presbyters, which some within the Church of England would find difficult to accept. However:

- As previously noted, the Church of England already implicitly recognises presbyteral confirmations in its permission for the performance of joint confirmation services.

- While, as we saw chapter 4, there are good reasons for the Church of England to retain ancient practice of bishops confirming (and for other churches to adopt the practice), it is difficult to see why it should regard presbyteral confirmations as absolutely invalid (as opposed to irregular).

As we have noted repeatedly in the course of this study, at the heart of confirmation is prayer. The reason why the laying on of hands in confirmation is important is that it signifies prayer that God will strengthen and defend the person being confirmed through the sevenfold gift of the Holy Spirit. If we ask why we believe that this prayer will be heard, the answer is that Jesus told us, 'If you then, who are evil, know how to give good gifts to your children, how much more will the heavenly Father give the Holy Spirit to those who ask him' (Luke 11:13).

The question the Church of England has to ask itself is whether it really believes that these words of Jesus only apply when it is a bishop who is doing the asking. It is true that in Acts 8 and 19 it is apostles who do the asking but today, is it bishops – and only bishops – who should be viewed as the successors of the apostles in this regard? Are there any biblical grounds for saying that God has restricted this aspect of apostolic ministry so absolutely to bishops as the successors of the apostles that he simply rules out confirmation prayers uttered by anyone else?

If there is no reason for thinking that this is the case, then the Church of England needs to be prepared to come off the fence and say unequivocally that it regards those confirmed by presbyters as truly confirmed and that therefore no further service of confirmation should be required in their case.

What is the challenge of confirmation to the individual?

The most important question raised by the Church of England's practice of confirmation is what it means in terms of individual response. What does mean for someone to respond rightly to confirmation? A helpful answer to this question is given by Colquhoun in what he writes about 'The Challenge of Confirmation'.

First of all, he says:

> Confirmation is a challenge to make a personal decision for Christ. It demands of the person confirmed a response of faith – free, deliberate, intelligent – to God's saving grace. No one can in fact be confirmed unless he professes to have made that response. This is the significance of the bishop's question at the outset of the service. The question concerns the ratification of the vows of baptism, and it receives from each of those to be confirmed a personal answer – *I do.*
>
> In making that answer the confirmee is saying in effect, 'I acknowledge myself to be

a disciple of Jesus Christ. I have heard his call, "Follow me." I have answered his call. I have repented and believe the gospel. Henceforth by God's help I will obey his will and live to his glory.'[17]

The second challenge of confirmation, Colquhoun says, is:

> in regards to the Church. It calls us to take our full place in the life of the Church as intelligent and instructed members: to share in its worship and rejoice in its fellowship all our day.
>
> (a) Churchmanship means *worship*. In a special sense it means the worship of Holy Communion, to the privilege of which the confirmed person is now admitted. Let him resolve to avail himself of this privilege regularly and gratefully. Sunday by Sunday the invitation is extended to him: 'Draw near with faith and take this holy sacrament to your comfort' and that invitation should never fail to meet with a ready and obedient response.
>
> (b) Churchmanship means service for Christ. We are made members of his body in baptism in order that we may serve him; and the commission to serve is given to us in confirmation. The laying on of hands by the bishop is almost like an act of

---

[17] Colquhoun, *Catechism and Confirmation*, 184.

ordination, a solemn setting apart for the Lord's work. It cannot be too strongly emphasised that while baptism admits to *membership* of the church, confirmation admits to *ministry* in the church – and every Christian is called upon to exercise some such ministry.

(c) Churchmanship means *learning*. I we want to worship and serve the Lord aright within the Church's fellowship we must have a firm and intelligent grasp of our faith. Preparation for confirmation involves receiving a certain amount of instruction in the Christian religion. But at the most this is no more than a beginning. It must not be allowed to end there. [18]

Thirdly, he says:

Confirmation is a challenge to the ongoing life of Christian discipleship. It is in fact a challenge to live for God day by day in the power of the Holy Spirit ... Is it possible to live victoriously and serve God faithfully in this sinful world?

The answer is, Yes, it is possible if we on our part do what is required of us. If, that is, we place ourselves unreservedly in God's hands, open our lives fully to the Holy Spirit, and walk obediently each day in the

---

[18] Colquhoun, *Catechism and Confirmation*, 185–87.

light of his Word. In the end, the victorious Christian life is a matter of keeping in touch with Jesus Christ within the fellowship of the Church and availing ourselves of God's grace by every means at our disposal.

The grace offered to us in confirmation is never withdrawn from us, but we must receive it continuously; we must co-operate with God. Paul urged Timothy to 'stir up' the gift of God that was within him by the laying on of hands (2 Tim 1:6 RV). So we must constantly rekindle the fire divine in our own lives.[19]

---

[19] Colquhoun, *Catechism and Confirmation,* 187–88.

Appendix A

The service of confirmation in *An English Prayer Book*.[1]

Confirmation

1. *The minister reads these words of* INTRODUCTION:

    Our church requires that all who come to confirmation should know and understand the Apostles' Creed, the Lord's Prayer and the Ten Commandments, and be able to answer the other questions in the catechism.

    When they come of age those baptized as infants may openly take upon themselves and confirm, before the people of God, the promises made in their name by their godparents. They should seek the help and grace of God to enable them to remain faithful to their profession of faith. This we urge those who come now to confirmation to do, praying that they would know the Holy Spirit as their strength and guide as they serve the Lord Jesus Christ.

2. *The bishop asks those who have come to confirmation:*

    Do you here in the presence of God and this congregation renew the solemn promises made in your name at your baptism? Do you confirm that you repent of your sins and renounce evil; that you sincerely believe and trust in Christ; and that you will faithfully obey God all the days of your life?

Answer   **I do.**

---

[1] Confirmation in *An English Prayer Book*, available at https://churchsociety.org/docs/english_prayer_book/17_EPB_confirmation.pdf.

Bishop	Let us pray that God will strengthen with his Holy Spirit these persons who now confirm their commitment to those promises made at their baptism and that they will serve Christ the Lord faithfully all their days.
	Our help is in the name of the Lord,
All	**who has made heaven and earth.**
Bishop	Blessed be the name of the Lord
All	**now and for evermore.**
Bishop	Lord, hear our prayer,
All	**And let our cry come to you.**

3. *The bishop continues in prayer:*

Almighty and everliving God,
by whose grace these your servants
have been born again of water and the Spirit
and have received forgiveness of all their sins:
strengthen them with the Holy Spirit the Comforter;
daily increase in them your gifts of grace;
the spirit of wisdom and understanding,
the spirit of guidance and strength,
the spirit of knowledge and true godliness,
and fill them, O Lord, with the spirit of your holy fear,
both now and for ever. **Amen.**

4. *Those who have come to confirmation kneel before the bishop. He lays his hand upon the head of each and prays:*

Defend, O Lord, your servant *N*
with your heavenly grace,
that *he* may continue yours for ever;
and daily increase in your Holy Spirit
until *he* comes to your eternal kingdom. **Amen.**

5. *Then the bishop says:*

           The Lord be with you.

All   **And with your spirit.**

Bishop   Let us pray.

6.   THE LORD'S PRAYER

Either

All

Our Father, who art in heaven, hallowed by thy name, thy kingdom come, thy will be done on earth as it is heaven. Give us this day our daily bread. And forgive us our trespasses as we forgive those who trespass against us. And lead us not into temptation but deliver us from evil. For thine is the kingdom, the power and the glory, for ever and ever. Amen.

Or

Our Father in heaven, hallowed by your name, your kingdom come, your will be done, on earth as it is in heaven. Give us today our daily bread. Forgive us our sins as we forgive those who sin against us. Lead us not into temptation but deliver us from evil. For yours is the kingdom, the power, and the glory, now and for ever. Amen

7.   *The bishop continues in prayer:*

      Almighty and ever-living God,
      you teach us both to intend and to do those things
      that are good and acceptable in your sight.
      We humbly pray for these your servants
      upon whom we have laid our hands,
      following the example of your holy apostles.
      Reassure them of your favour and goodness;
      let your fatherly hand always be over them;

> may your Holy Spirit be ever with them;
> lead them into all truth;
> and teach them to obey your Word
> so that in the end they obtain eternal life;
> through Jesus Christ our Lord. **Amen.**

8.

All **Almighty and everlasting God,**
be pleased, we pray,
to direct, sanctify,
and govern our hearts and bodies
so that we will keep your laws
and obey your commands;
and grant that through y our mighty protection
we may be preserved in body and soul,
both here and for ever,
through our Lord and Saviour Jesus Christ. Amen.

9. *The bishop prays for those who have come to confirmation:*

> The blessing of God Almighty, the Father, the Son, and the Holy Spirit, be upon you, and remain with you for ever. **Amen**

No persons shall be admitted to the Holy Communion until they have been confirmed, or have been prepared for confirmation and wish to be confirmed.

APPENDIX B

ADMISSION OF BAPTISED CHILDREN TO HOLY COMMUNION REGULATIONS 2006[1]

The General Synod hereby makes the following Regulations under paragraph 1(c) of Canon B15A:

1. These Regulations may be cited as the Admission of Baptised Children to Holy Communion Regulations 2006 and shall come into force on the fifteenth day of June 2006 as appointed by the Archbishops of Canterbury and York.

2. Children who have been baptised but who have not yet been confirmed and who are not yet ready and desirous to be confirmed as required by paragraph 1(a) of Canon B15A may be admitted to Holy Communion provided that the conditions set out in these Regulations are satisfied.

3. Every diocesan bishop may at any time make a direction to the effect that applications from parishes under these Regulations may be made in his diocese. The bishop's discretion in this respect shall be absolute, and he may at any time revoke such a direction (without prejudice to the validity of any permissions already granted thereunder).

4. Where a direction under paragraph 3 is in force in a diocese, an incumbent may apply to the bishop for permission that children falling within the definition in paragraph 2 may be admitted to Holy Communion in one or more of the parishes

---

[1] Admission of Baptised Children to Holy Communion Regulations 2006, available at: http://www.rochester.anglican.org/content/pages/documents/1426514910.pdf.

in the incumbent's charge. Such application must be made in writing and must be accompanied by a copy of a resolution in support of the application passed by the parochial church council of each parish in respect of which the application is made.

5. Before granting any permission under paragraph 4, the bishop must first satisfy himself (a) that the parish concerned has made adequate provision for preparation and continuing nurture in the Christian life and will encourage any child admitted to Holy Communion under these Regulations to be confirmed at the appropriate time and (b) where the parish concerned is within the area of a local ecumenical project established under Canon B 44, that the other participating Churches have been consulted.

6. The bishop's decision in relation to any application under paragraph 4 shall be final, but a refusal shall not prevent a further application being made on behalf of the parish concerned, provided that at least one year has elapsed since the most recent previous application was refused.

7. Any permission granted under paragraph 4 shall remain in force unless and until revoked by the bishop. The bishop must revoke such permission upon receipt of an application for the purpose made by the incumbent. Such application must be made in writing and accompanied by a copy of a resolution in support of the application passed by the parochial church council of each parish in respect of which the application is made. Otherwise, the bishop may only revoke a permission granted under paragraph 4 if he considers that the conditions specified in paragraph 5 are no longer being satisfactorily discharged. Before revoking any permission on these grounds, the bishop shall first notify the incumbent of his concerns in

writing and shall afford the incumbent a reasonable time to respond and, where appropriate, to take remedial action.

8. Where a permission granted under paragraph 4 is in force, the incumbent shall not admit any child to Holy Communion unless he or she is satisfied that (a) the child has been baptised and (b) a person having parental responsibility for the child is content that the child should be so admitted. Otherwise, subject to any direction of the bishop, it is within the incumbent's absolute discretion to decide whether, and if so when, any child should first be admitted to Holy Communion.

9. The incumbent shall maintain a register of all children admitted to Holy Communion under these Regulations, and where practicable will record on the child's baptismal certificate the date and place of the child's first admission. If the baptismal certificate is not available, the incumbent shall present the child with a separate certificate recording the same details.

10. A child who presents evidence in the form stipulated in paragraph 9 that he or she has been admitted to Holy Communion under these Regulations shall be so admitted at any service of Holy Communion conducted according to the rites of the Church of England in any place, regardless of whether or not any permission under paragraph 4 is in force in that place or was in force in that place until revoked.

11. These Regulations shall apply to a cathedral as if it were a parish, with the modifications that:

(a) any application under paragraphs 3 or 7 must be made by the dean of the cathedral concerned, accompanied by a copy of a resolution in support of the application passed by the chapter of the cathedral concerned;

(b) the obligations imposed on the incumbent under paragraphs 8 and 9 shall be imposed on the dean of the cathedral concerned.

12. A diocesan bishop may delegate any of his functions under these Regulations (except his functions under paragraph 3) to a person appointed by him for the purpose, being a suffragan or assistant bishop or archdeacon of the diocese.

13. In these Regulations:

(a) 'incumbent', in relation to a parish, includes:

(i) in a case where the benefice concerned is vacant (and paragraph (ii) below does not apply), the rural dean;

(ii) in a case where a suspension period (within the meaning of the Pastoral Measure 1983) applies to the benefice concerned, the priest-in-charge; and

(iii) in a case where a special cure of souls in respect of the parish has been assigned to a vicar in a team ministry by a Scheme under the Pastoral Measure 1983 or by licence from the bishop, that vicar; and

(b) references to paragraph numbers are to the relevant paragraph or paragraphs in these Regulations.

Other Latimer Publications

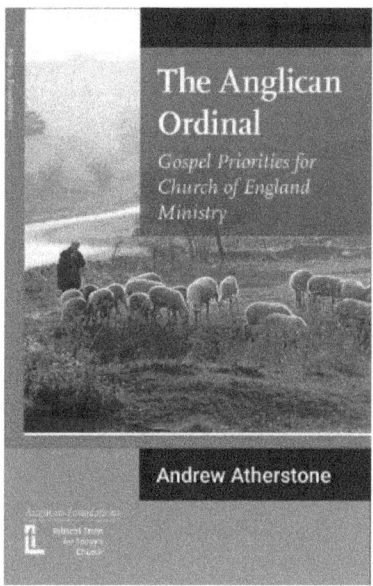

This book is part of our *Anglican Foundation* series, which offer practical guidance on Church of England services.

There is no better handbook for Anglican ministry than the Anglican ordinal – the authorized liturgy for ordaining new ministers. The ordinal contains a beautiful, succinct description of theological priorities and ministry models for today's Church. This booklet offers a simple exposition of the ordinal's primary themes. Anglican clergy are called to public ministry as messengers, sentinels, stewards, and shepherds. They are asked searching questions and they make solemn promises. The Holy Spirit's anointing is invoked upon their ministries, with the laying-on-of-hands, and they are gifted a Bible as the visual symbol of their new pastoral and preaching office. This booklet is a handy primer for ordinands and clergy, and all those responsible for their selection, training, and deployment.

Whilst Common Worship (2000) provides a Book of Common Prayer Communion (BCP) in modern English, sadly there is no such provision for the BCP baptism service. For some Anglican evangelicals this may not seem to be a particularly regrettable omission.

There are those who might not be persuaded of the biblical mandate for baptising infants, whilst others might have concerns over some of the language used that may appear to affirm 'baptismal regeneration'. This booklet is an attempt not only to engage with those questions and concerns but also to proffer an enthusiastic support for the theology and liturgical content of the BCP Baptism service. It has a great emphasis on the covenantal grace of God which encourages Christian parents to "doubt not – but earnestly believe" in God's faithfulness and mercy. In so doing it directs our primary focus to our promise keeping God and not to ourselves.

Are bishops biblical? As fissures emerge within the worldwide Anglican communion, the principle and praxis of episcopacy have never been more pertinent. For some Anglicans, bishops are essential for the church. For others, they are something of a necessary evil; baggage from the English reformation that we might be better off without.

These concerns are nothing new. In the seventeenth century, debates surrounding the validity and authority of bishops abounded. Into those debates wrote James Ussher, archbishop of Armagh and Primate of All Ireland. Ussher was a remarkable figure: a preeminent historian, biblical scholar, and theologian, respected by English puritans and Irish Jesuits alike. As is often the case with such luminaries, various camps have claimed Ussher as their own; whether they be **puritan, high church, or anglo-catholic.**

By studying Ussher's ecclesiastical career and his two works on church government, this study assesses Ussher's episcopalian convictions, particularly regarding the validity and authority of bishops. In doing so, it hopes to reintroduce Ussher to the evangelical Anglican world, and demonstrate that episcopacy is not a necessary evil, but a force for good in the church of God.

After three and a half centuries of relative neglect, the Church of England embarked on a thoroughgoing reform of its Canons, which led to the promulgation of an entirely new series of them in 1964 and in 1969. A year later, the present General Synod was inaugurated, and since then the Church's canon law has undergone a sometimes bewildering number of additions and alterations.

Keeping track of these developments is not easy, because although the material is available, until now it has not been gathered together in one place or set out in a user-friendly format. This book is a compilation of the 1964/1969 Canons with all their many modifications in the first half-century of their existence. It has no legal authority of its own, and those wanting to know what Canons are currently in force will need to consult the official publications of the Church of England.

This edition is a reference work aimed to clarify how the Church has developed its Canons over the past fifty years. As such, it will be of great benefit to historians, and to lawmakers in the Church who want to find out what has happened to the Canons in the recent past, even as they make new ones for the future. It is a snapshot taken in 2020 that provides a template for the study of a work that is still in progress, even as it continues to reflect the principles and practices that have guided its development since 1970.

Lightning Source UK Ltd.
Milton Keynes UK
UKHW011244080422
401275UK00001B/57